Lincoln on Black and White:
A Documentary History

PUBLISHER'S NOTE

Re: Zilversmit - Lincoln on Black and White

Please note that Introduction and Preface are inadvertent
duplications.

Lincoln on Black and White:
A Documentary History

Arthur Zilversmit
Lake Forest College

Editor

ROBERT E. KRIEGER PUBLISHING COMPANY
MALABAR, FLORIDA
1983

Original Edition 1971
Reprint Edition 1983 w/ new Introduction

Printed and Published by
ROBERT E. KRIEGER PUBLISHING COMPANY, INC.
KRIEGER DRIVE
MALABAR, FLORIDA 32950

Printed in the United States of America

Library of Congress Cataloging in Publication Data
Main entry under title:

Lincoln on black and white.

   Reprint. Originally published: Belmont, Calif.:
Wadsworth Pub. Co., 1971.
   Bibliography: p.
   1. Lincoln, Abraham, 1808-1865—Views on slavery. 2. Lincoln, Abraham, 1809-1865—Views on Afro-Americans. 3. Slavery—United States—History—Sources. 4. Afro-Americans—History—Sources. 5. United States—History—Civil War, 1861-1865—Sources. I. Zilversmit, Arthur.
E457.92   1983   973.7′092′4   83-6184
ISBN 0-89874-633-7

For Charlotte, Marc, and Karen

"Didn't you do any history, at school?"
"I attended history lessons. It is not the same thing."[1]

[1]Josephine Tey, *The Daughter of Time* (New York: Berkley Publishing Corp., 1959), p. 32.

Introduction

The shadow of Abraham Lincoln looms large over a crucial period of American history. The period in which this nation came to grips with the problem of human slavery was presided over by a man who was born in a border state and became head of a political party dominated by the Northern states. Just as Lincoln by birth represented the slave-holding states and by election represented the free states, so his historical reputation on the race issue has led to conflicting interpretations. On the one hand, we have the textbook story of Lincoln as "The Great Emancipator;" on the other hand, we have the verdict of a black historian, Lerone Bennett, Jr., that Lincoln was the "embodiment, not the transcendence, of the American tradition, which is...a racist tradition."[1]

Was Lincoln a racist? More important, how did Lincoln's racial views affect the course of our history? Professional historians differ markedly in their views on Lincoln's posture on race. James G. Rhodes, in his multivolume history of the United States, maintains that Lincoln had been consistently anti-slavery and that tempering his opposition to slavery with "Anglo-Saxon caution," he issued the Emancipation Proclamation at precisely the right moment.[2] But J.G. Randall, author of the most authoritative history of the Lincoln presidency, depicts Lincoln as being anti-slavery in only the most cautious manner and claims that Lincoln's general views on race differed hardly at all from those of his Democratic opponent, Stephen A. Douglas. Randall's Lincoln reluctantly came to the conclusion that the Emancipation Proclamation was necessary but, Randall maintains, this radical step marked an unfortunate departure from Lincoln's characteristic conservative approach.[3]

---

[1]Lerone Bennett, Jr., "Was Lincoln a White Supremacist?" *Ebony*, XXIII (February 1968), p. 42.

[2]James G. Rhodes, *History of the United States from the Compromise of 1850*, 8 vol. (New York: Harper and Brothers and the Macmillan Company, 1893-1919), II, p. 310; III, pp. 633-635; IV, p. 215.

[3]J.G. Randall, *Lincoln the President*, 4 vols. (4th vol. completed by Richard Current) (New York: Dodd, Mead & Co., 1945-1955), I., pp. 123, 181-182, and *passim*.

Allan Nevins, one of the most respected historians of his day, concedes that Lincoln issued the Proclamation out of necessity rather than moral conviction but, Nevins maintains, Lincoln fully recognized and accepted the revolutionary implications of his act. While Randall holds that the Proclamation resulted only in "a limping freedom," Nevins declares that it "irrevocably committed the United States. . . to the early eradication of slavery. . . Lincoln had converted the war into a struggle for the rights of labor in the broadest sense."[4]

Benjamin Quarles, one of the nation's leading black historians, is basically sympathetic to Lincoln. Quarles' Lincoln moved slowly, but he did develop a deep hatred for slavery. Although he did not favor Negro equality, "Lincoln was not anti-Negro. . . despite the strong racial prejudices so prevalent where he lived." Although the decision to emancipate the slaves was thrust upon Lincoln, "by the time he announced it to the world, it had become an integral part of his own thinking."[5]

While professional historians do not accept the story of "The Great Emancipator" as it has been passed down in folklore, Benjamin Thomas, author of a highly-regarded one volume biography of Lincoln, depicts him as a man who, while not always a firm opponent of slavery, ultimately can understand Lincoln's racial views. Thomas argues, only by realizing that Lincoln had a unique capacity for personal growth and learning. that Lincoln had a unique capacity for personal growth and learning. Unlike Randall, Thomas maintains that by the time of the debates with Douglas, there *was* a great difference in their racial views. He minimizes his hero's well-known statements on Negro inequality by arguing that Lincoln made them only after he had been relentlessly badgered by Douglas.[6]

Lincoln's most recent biographer, Stephen B. Oates, also defends his subject's racial record. But while the key to understanding Thomas' Lincoln is the idea of growth and a developing antipathy to slavery, Oates claims that Lincoln was an anti-slavery man from his earliest days. As President, however, Oates suggests, Lincoln had to temper his personal feelings out of respect for the Constitution as well as a practical need to

---

[4]Allan Nevins, *The War for the Union,* 2 vols. (New York: Charles Scribner's Sons, 1959-1960), II, pp. 236-237.

[5]Benjamin Quarles, *Lincoln and the Negro* (New York: Oxford University Press, 1962), pp. 36, 139.

[6]Benjamin Thomas, *Abraham Lincoln* (New York: Alfred A. Knopf, 1953), pp. 188, 192.

keep the border states loyal to the Union. Lincoln, as Oates depicts him, comes close to the classic picture of "The Great Emancipator."[7]

In the 1960's, as the nation increasingly confronted its racial problems, historians renewed their interest in Lincoln's racial views. Bennett's article of 1968 encouraged a flurry of responses. The best of these succeeded in providing new insights into the complexities of the issues. George Frederickson, for example, shows how a careful re-reading of Lincoln's own words during the debates with Douglas can shed new light on their meaning and Don E. Fehrenbacher, an eminent Lincoln historian, cautions us to view Lincoln's "racist" remarks within their historical context.[8]

Recent historical interest in Reconstruction policies has led to a re-examination of the vital question—what would Lincoln have done if he had lived to face the problems of reconstruction? Peyton McCrary argues that just before the assassination, the President was ready to accept a radical policy on the controversial issue of Negro suffrage. He depicts Lincoln as being, above all, a political realist. Therefore, he argues, "As a pragmatic politician, if not as a man with a commitment to social justice for the freedmen, Lincoln could hardly have escaped the conclusion that at the end of the war there was nowhere to go but to the left." If Lincoln had lived he would have joined the radical members of his party in devising ways to protect the rights of the newly freed blacks.[9]

Which of these Lincolns was the real one? The answer to this question is as complex as any in historical intrepretation. The first step in answering it involves an analysis of what Lincoln actually said and did. In order to allow readers to reach their own conclusions about Lincoln, I have assembled a varied, representative collection of Lincoln's writings. I have also included statements by his contemporaries to provide a glimpse of the context within which Lincoln thought, spoke, and acted.

While examining what Lincoln actually said, readers will confront the fundamental questions that lie at the heart of historical judgments. To

---

[7]Stephen B. Oates, *With Malice Toward None: The Life of Abraham Lincoln* (New York: Harper, 1977), pp. 37-39.

[8]George Frederickson, "A Man but Not a Brother: Abraham Lincoln and Racial Equality," *Journal of Southern History,* 41 (1975), 46-48; Don E. Fehrenbacher, "Only His Stepchildren: Lincoln and the Negro," *Civil War History,* 20 (1974) 303.

[9]Peyton McCrary, *Abraham Lincoln and Reconstruction: The Louisiana Experiment* (Princeton, N.J.: Princeton University Press, 1978), pp. xi, xii, 9, 11, 210, 356. LaWanda Cox, *Lincoln and Black Freedom: A Study in Presidential Leadership* (Columbia, S. C.: University of South Carolina Press, 1981) strongly supports McCrary's view.

begin with, we must deal with a technical question: how can we reconcile the apparent contradictions in the evidence? Are all the documents equally valid? Although the documents focus on a limited group of issues, a study of Lincoln's views on slavery and race can bring us to a fuller understanding of Lincoln as a man and as a political leader. Lincoln's attempts to deal with the slavery question in a political context can give us some insight into the relationship of pragmatic democratic politics and deeply-felt moral issues. The documents raise fundamental questions not only about the capacity of our political system to deal with moral questions, but also about the nature of leadership within a democratic system: to what degree must leaders follow public opinion? To what extent can they transcend the views of their neighbors (who elected them) and assume a leadership role? More philosophical issues that historians must deal with include such basic questions as the role of people in making history: to what degree is history shaped by human desires and actions, and to what degree are people—even great leaders—molded by history? The documents raise another fundamental historiographical question—the role of moral judgments in history. Should people of the past be judged by the standards of their times, or must historians use the moral values of their own times in evaluating historical figures? Moving beyond questions of moral judgment, to what degree are historians' perception of the past a product of their understanding of the present? Can the historians transcend the world-view of their age in trying to recapture that of another age?

For each reader, the documents will raise new questions because each of us confronts them from an individual perspective. To the extent the documents raise new questions, they will have performed their function of allowing readers to make their own historical judgments—to study history in the ways that historians do.

When historians approach the past, they see themselves as doing something different from the usual definitions of the study of history. In schools, the study of history usually means becoming familiar with the "facts" of history through studying a textbook and listening to lectures. It is difficult, under these circumstances, for students to realize that history is something more than a recounting of the events of the past; that history, is (in the words of a recent book on the subject) *"the act of selecting, analyzing, and writing about the past."* As James Davidson and Mark Lytle go on to say: "It is something that is done, that is constructed, rather than an inert body of data . . . something quite different than merely reporting 'the facts.'"[10]

---

[10]James West Davidson and Mark Hamilton Lytle, *After the Fact: The Art of Historical Detection* (New York, 1982), p. xvii.

Although students are sometimes asked to supplement their understanding of the "facts of the past" by "doing" some history of their own—that is, examining source materials and coming to their own conclusions about the events of the past, this is often impossible. Many students do not have access to a research library, and term paper projects can put a small library under great strain. This volume is, therefore, designed to offer readers direct access to primary source materials on an important issue in a convenient format. My object is to place readers in a situation where, on a limited and manageable scale, they can *be* historians, engaging in the process of understanding the past by evaluating much of the available evidence on Lincoln's racial views for themselves. By involving the reader in the *process* of history, I hope not only to share the historian's excitement in evaluating evidence but to help provide a basis by which readers can judge the work of other historians. For it is only by developing an understanding of how historians evaluate evidence and present their conclusions that we can judge their works.

In most cases I have let the documents speak for themselves, and I have resisted the temptation to provide elaborate notes explaining what readers can determine for themselves by careful reading of the document. Accordingly, for most documents I have provided only a statement about its source. For documents that have been reprinted, I have also indicated the location of the original. By examining the source of the document, the reader may reach a conclusion about its significance or even its authenticity.

Because of the immense amount of material on this subject, I have had to make deletions in most of the documents, but in no case do these deletions change the essential meaning of the statement. Deletions within a paragraph are designated by the use of elipses (...). When an entire paragraph or more has been deleted I have used five dots (.....) to indicate the omission.

Lake Forest College
May 22, 1983

Preface

The shadow of Abraham Lincoln looms large over a crucial period of American history. The period in which this nation came to grips with the problem of human slavery was presided over by a man who was born in a border state and became head of a political party dominated by the Northern states. Just as Lincoln by birth represented the slave-holding states and by election represented the free states, so his historical reputation on the race issue has led to conflicting interpretations. On the one hand we have the textbook story of Lincoln as "The Great Emancipator"; on the other hand we have the verdict of a black historian, Lerone Bennet, Jr., that Lincoln was the "embodiment, not the transcendence, of the American tradition, which is . . . a racist tradition." [1]

Was Lincoln a racist? More important, how did Lincoln's racial views affect the course of our history? Professional historians differ markedly in their views on Lincoln's posture on race. James G. Rhodes, in his multivolume history of the United States, maintains that Lincoln had been consistently anti-slavery and that tempering his opposition to slavery with "Anglo-Saxon caution," he issued the Emancipation Proclamation at precisely the right moment.[2] But J. G. Randall, author of the most authoritative history of the Lincoln presidency, depicts Lincoln as being anti-slavery in only the most cautious manner and claims that Lincoln's general views on race differed hardly at all from those of his Democratic opponent, Stephen A. Douglas. Randall's Lincoln reluctantly came to the conclusion that the Emancipation Proclamation was necessary but, Randall maintains, this rad-

[1] Lerone Bennett, Jr., "Was Lincoln a White Supremacist?" *Ebony,* XXIII (February 1968), p. 42.

[2] James G. Rhodes, *History of the United States from the Compromise of 1850,* 8 vols. (New York: Harper and Brothers and the Macmillan Company, 1893–1919), II, p. 310; III, pp. 633–635; IV, p. 215.

ical step marked an unfortunate departure from Lincoln's characteristic conservative approach.[3]

Allan Nevins, one of the most respected historians of our day, concedes that Lincoln issued the Proclamation out of necessity rather than moral conviction but, Nevins maintains, Lincoln fully recognized and accepted the revolutionary implications of his act. While Randall holds that the Proclamation resulted only in "a limping freedom," Nevins declares that it "irrevocably committed the United States . . . to the early eradication of slavery. . . . Lincoln had converted the war into a struggle for the rights of labor in the broadest sense." [4]

Although professional historians do not accept the story of "The Great Emancipator" as it has been passed down to us in folklore, Benjamin Thomas, author of the best single-volume biography of Lincoln, depicts Lincoln as deeply committed to the position that slavery was immoral and should be eradicated. Unlike Randall, Thomas maintains that there was a great difference in the racial views of Lincoln and Douglas and he minimizes Lincoln's statements on Negro inequality by pointing out that Lincoln made them only after he had been relentlessly badgered by Douglas.[5]

Benjamin Quarles, one of the nation's leading black historians, is basically sympathetic to Lincoln. Quarles' Lincoln moved slowly, but he did develop a deep hatred for slavery. Although he did not favor Negro equality, "Lincoln was not anti-Negro . . . despite the strong racial prejudices so prevalent where he lived." Despite the fact that Emancipation was thrust upon Lincoln, "by the time he announced it to the world, it had become an integral part of his own thinking." [6]

Which of these Lincolns was the real one? The answer to this question is as complex as any in historical interpretation. The first step in answering it involves an analysis of what Lincoln actually

---

[3] J. G. Randall, *Lincoln the President,* 4 vols. (4th vol. completed by Richard Current) (New York: Dodd, Mead & Co., 1945–1955), I, pp. 123, 181–182, and *passim.*

[4] Allan Nevins, *The War for the Union,* 2 vols. (New York: Charles Scribner's Sons, 1959–1960), II, pp. 236–237.

[5] Benjamin Thomas, *Abraham Lincoln* (New York: Alfred A. Knopf, 1953), pp. 188, 192.

[6] Benjamin Quarles, *Lincoln and the Negro* (New York: Oxford University Press, 1962), pp. 36, 139.

said and did. In order to allow the reader to reach his own conclusions about Lincoln, I have assembled a varied, representative collection of Lincoln's writings. I have also included statements by his contemporaries to provide a glimpse of the context within which Lincoln thought, spoke, and acted.

While reading what Lincoln said, the reader will confront the fundamental questions that lie at the heart of historical judgments. To begin with, we must deal with a technical question: how can we reconcile the apparent contradictions in the evidence? Are all the documents equally valid? Although the documents focus on a limited group of issues, a study of Lincoln's views on slavery and race can bring us to a fuller understanding of Lincoln as a man and as a political leader. Lincoln's attempts to deal with the slavery question in a political context can give us some insight into the relationship of pragmatic democratic politics and deeply-felt moral issues. The documents raise fundamental questions not only about the capacity of our political system to deal with moral questions, but also about the nature of leadership within a democratic system: to what degree must a leader follow public opinion? To what extent can he transcend the views of his neighbors (who elected him) and assume a leadership role? More philosophical issues that the historian must deal with include such basic questions as the role of men in making history: to what degree is history shaped by men, and to what degree are men—even great men—molded by history? The documents raise another fundamental historiographical question—the role of moral judgments in history. Can men of the past be judged exclusively by the standards of their times, or must the historian use the moral values of his own time in evaluating historical figures? Moving beyond questions of moral judgment, to what degree is the historian's perception of the past a product of his understanding of the present? Can the historian transcend the world-view of his age in trying to recapture that of another age?

The documents will raise other questions; each reader confronts them anew, from his own perspective. To the degree the following documents raise new questions, they will have performed their function of allowing each reader to be "his own historian."

In most cases the documents speak for themselves, and I have resisted the temptation to provide elaborate notes explaining what the reader can determine for himself by a careful reading of the document. Accordingly, for most documents I have provided only a statement about its source. For documents that have been reprinted, I have also indicated the location of the original. By examining the source of the document the reader may reach a conclusion about its significance or even its authenticity.

Because of the immense amount of material on this subject, I have had to make deletions in most of the documents, but in no case do these deletions change the essential meaning of the statement. Deletions within a paragraph are designated by the use of elipses. When an entire paragraph or more has been deleted I have used five dots to indicate the omission.

This book has benefited greatly from the incisive criticism of three historians who have managed the difficult task of being both good friends and discerning critics. Jack M. Holl, University of Washington, and Leon F. Litwack, University of California, Berkeley, helped me to recast the introduction, and Robert McColley, University of Illinois, Urbana-Champaign, directed me towards several important documents. I want to thank Kevin Riordan and Robert Gormley, Wadsworth Publishing Company, for their help in developing this series. I am grateful to Lake Forest College and the Ford Foundation for providing released time from teaching while I pursued this project. My wife, Charlotte, provided both essential moral support and essential prodding—God knows both were needed.

Contents

One   The Early Years (1837–1849)   *1*

1. Protest in Illinois Legislature on Slavery, March 3, 1837   *3*
2. To Mary Speed, September 27, 1841   *4*
3. To Williamson Durley, October 3, 1845   *5*
4. Lincoln and the Matson Negroes, 1847   *7*
5. Remarks and Resolution Introduced in United States House of Representatives Concerning Abolition of Slavery in the District of Columbia, January 10, 1849   *9*

Two   The Sectional Crisis (1854–1860)   *13*

6. Speech at Peoria, Illinois, October 16, 1854   *14*
7. Henry A. Groves to Abraham Lincoln, November 18, 1854   *22*
8. To George Robertson, August 15, 1855   *24*
9. To Joshua F. Speed, August 24, 1855   *25*
10. Speech at Springfield, Illinois, June 26, 1857   *27*
11. "A House Divided": Speech at Springfield, Illinois, June 16, 1858   *31*
12. Speech at Chicago, Illinois, July 10, 1858   *34*
13. First Debate with Stephen A. Douglas at Ottawa, Illinois, August 21, 1858   *39*
14. Second Debate with Stephen A. Douglas at Freeport, Illinois, August 27, 1858   *43*
15. Speech at Carlinville, Illinois, August 31, 1858   *46*
16. Fourth Debate with Stephen A. Douglas at Charleston, Illinois, September 18, 1858   *47*

17. Fifth Debate with Stephen A. Douglas at Galesburg, Illinois, October 7, 1858   *51*

18. Seventh and Last Debate with Stephen A. Douglas at Alton, Illinois, October 15, 1858   *55*

19. To Elihu B. Washburne, January 29, 1859   *59*

20. To Salmon P. Chase, June 9, 1859   *60*

21. Speech at Cincinnati, Ohio, September 17, 1859   *61*

22. Speech at New Haven, Connecticut, March 6, 1860   *63*

23. Speech of H. Ford Douglass, July 4, 1860   *64*

Three   The Presidency: Colonization and Emancipation (1860–1863)   *69*

24. Frederick Douglass: "The Late Election," December, 1860   *70*

25. To Elihu B. Washburne, December 13, 1860   *74*

26. To Henry J. Raymond, December 18, 1860   *75*

27. To William H. Seward, February 1, 1861   *76*

28. To John C. Frémont, September 2, 1861   *77*

29. To Orville H. Browning, September 22, 1861   *78*

30. Annual Message to Congress, December 3, 1861   *80*

31. Message to Congress, March 6, 1862   *82*

32. To Horace Greeley, March 24, 1862   *83*

33. Message to Congress, April 16, 1862   *84*

34. Proclamation Revoking General Hunter's Order of Military Emancipation of May 9, 1862, May 19, 1962   *85*

35. Appeal to Border State Representatives to Favor Compensated Emancipation, July 12, 1862   *87*

36. To the Senate and House of Representatives, July 14, 1862   *89*

37. Second Confiscation Act, July 17, 1862   *89*

38. Diary of Salmon P. Chase, July 21, 1862; July 22, 1862; August 3, 1862   *91*

39. Remarks to Deputation of Western Gentlemen, August 4, 1862   *94*

40. Address on Colonization to a Deputation of Negroes, August 14, 1862   *95*

41. Frederick Douglass: "The President and His Speeches," September 1862   *100*

42. Horace Greeley: "The Prayer of Twenty Millions," August 19, 1862   *103*

43. To Horace Greeley, August 22, 1862   *107*

44. Reply to Emancipation Memorial Presented by Chicago Christians of All Denominations, September 13, 1862   *108*

45. Diary of Salmon P. Chase, September 22, 1862   *111*

46. Preliminary Emancipation Proclamation, September 22, 1862   *113*

47. Frederick Douglass, "Emancipation Proclaimed," October, 1862   *116*

48. Annual Message to Congress, December 1, 1862   *118*

49. William A. Richardson: "The President's Message" (Speech in the House of Representatives), December 8, 1862   *122*

50. Speech of James Brooks, December 30, 1862   *126*

51. Emancipation Proclamation, January 1, 1863   *131*

52. Frederick Douglass, "The Proclamation and a Negro Army," February, 1863   *133*

Four   The Presidency: Emancipation and Reconstruction (1863–1865)   *139*

53. To John A. McClernand, January 8, 1863   *140*

54. To Andrew Johnson, March 26, 1863   *141*

55. To Nathaniel P. Banks, August 5, 1863   *142*

56. To Ulysses S. Grant, August 9, 1863   *144*

57. Frederick Douglass, "The Black Man at the White House," August 10, 1863   *145*

58. To James C. Conkling, August 26, 1863   *148*

59. To Salmon P. Chase, September 2, 1863   *151*

60. Annual Message to Congress, December 8, 1863   *152*

61. Proclamation of Amnesty and Reconstruction, December 8, 1863   *155*

62. John R. Eden, "Reconstruction" (Speech in the House of Representatives), February 27, 1864   *157*

63. To James S. Wadsworth, January, 1864 (?)   *160*

64. To James S. Wadsworth, January, 1864 (?) *161*

65. To John A. J. Creswell, March 7, 1864 *161*

66. To Michael Hahn, March 13, 1864 *163*

67. To John A. J. Creswell, March 17, 1864 *163*

68. To Albert G. Hodges, April 4, 1864 *164*

69. Reply to Committee Notifying Lincoln of His Renomination, June 9, 1864 *166*

70. From Charles D. Robinson, August 7, 1864 *168*

71. To Charles D. Robinson, August 17, 1864 *169*

72. Speech of the Rev. Mr. S. W. Chase Presenting a Bible from the Loyal Colored Residents of Baltimore to President Lincoln, September 7, 1865 *171*

73. To Henry W. Hoffman, October 10, 1864 *172*

74. Annual Message to Congress, December 6, 1864 *173*

75. To William H. Seward, January 31, 1865 *175*

76. Response to a Serenade, February 1, 1865 *176*

77. To the Senate and House of Representatives, February 5, 1865 *178*

78. To John Glenn, February 7, 1865 *179*

79. Second Inaugural Address, March 4, 1865 *180*

80. Salmon P. Chase to Abraham Lincoln, April 11, 1865 *182*

81. Last Public Address, April 11, 1865 *183*

Suggestions for Further Research *186*

Lincoln on Black and White:
A Documentary History

ONE

The Early
Years (1837–1849)

Abraham Lincoln was born in a slave state, but neither his father nor most of the other small farmers in that part of Kentucky owned slaves. By the time he was seven, Lincoln had moved to Indiana. Both Indiana and Illinois, Lincoln's home after 1830, were free states, yet both were extremely hostile to Negroes and had black codes which severely limited the rights of free Negroes and attempted to prevent the further immigration of blacks. Moreover, Lincoln's midwestern neighbors, many of whom had been born in the slave states, were vehemently opposed to abolitionism. Although a few men dared to be abolitionists, the example of Elijah Lovejoy, who was martyred at Alton, Illinois, in 1837 while defending his anti-slavery press, pointed to the dangers of an open avowal of abolitionist principles.

In 1828 and again in 1831 Lincoln saw slavery at first hand when he made the long trip down the Mississippi River to New Orleans. According to folklore, on his second trip, Lincoln was so distressed at the sight of a slave auction in New Orleans that he declared: "If I ever get a chance to hit that thing, I'll hit it hard." The source for this story, John Hanks, was not in New Orleans with Lincoln, and therefore most historians doubt the legend's authenticity.

When Lincoln made his debut in politics with his election to the lower house of the state legislature in 1834, slavery was not a prominent political issue. But when he was elected to Congress in 1846, the Mexican War brought the issue of the expansion of slave territory before the nation. Moreover, fifteen years of intense abolitionist agitation had made the question of the federal government's relation to slavery and the slave trade in the District of Columbia an important issue.

1

1

Protest in Illinois Legislature on Slavery[1]

March 3, 1837

The following protest was presented to the House, which was read and ordered to be spread on the journals, to wit:

"Resolutions upon the subject of domestic slavery having passed both branches of the General Assembly at its present session, the undersigned hereby protest against the passage of the same.[2]

---

[1] *House Journal,* Tenth General Assembly, First Session, pp. 817–818, in *The Collected Works of Abraham Lincoln,* Roy P. Basler *et al.,* eds., 9 vols. (New Brunswick, N. J.: Rutgers University Press, 1955), I, pp. 74–75.

[2] The General Assembly had received from the States of Virginia, Alabama, Mississippi, New York, and Connecticut "Memorials . . . relative to the existence of domestic slavery . . ." A joint select committee of both houses reported to the House on January 12, 1837, deeply deploring "the unfortunate condition of our fellow men, whose lots are cast in thraldom in a land of liberty and peace," but holding that "the arm of the General Government has no power to strike their fetters from them," and spurning indignantly "an interference with the rights of property in other States." Following a diatribe against abolition societies, the committee recommended the adoption of the following resolutions:

"*Resolved by the General Assembly of the State of Illinois,* That we highly disapprove of the formation of abolition societies, and of the doctrines promulgated by them.

"*Resolved,* That the right of property in slaves, is sacred to the slaveholding States by the Federal Constitution, and that they cannot be deprived of that right without their consent.

"*Resolved,* That the General Government cannot abolish slavery in the District of Columbia, against the consent of the citizens of said District without a manifest breach of good faith.

"*Resolved,* That the Governor be requested to transmit to the States of Virginia, Alabama, Mississippi, New York, and Connecticut, a copy of the foregoing report and resolutions." (*Ibid.,* pp. 243–244.)

Considerable debate ensued and numerous amendments were offered, but no details of the debate, nor details of the amendments, are recorded in the *Journal* except those offered from the floor on the final reporting of the resolutions. Lincoln moved to amend the amendment proposed by the committee to the third resolution by inserting after the word "Congress," the following: "Unless the people of the said District petition for the same." The motion failed and after further debate the resolutions "as amended" were finally passed by the

---

They believe that the institution of slavery is founded on both injustice and bad policy; but that the promulgation of abolition doctrines tends rather to increase than to abate its evils.

They believe that the Congress of the United States has no power, under the constitution, to interfere with the institution of slavery in the different States.

They believe that the Congress of the United States has the power, under the constitution, to abolish slavery in the District of Columbia; but that that power ought not to be exercised unless at the request of the people of said District.

The difference between these opinions and those contained in the said resolutions, is their reason for entering this protest."

DAN STONE,

A. LINCOLN,

Representatives from the county of Sangamon.

House on January 20. The Senate concurred on January 25. The resolutions as amended are not printed in the *Journal of the House,* but the degree to which the general sentiment of the resolutions was modified seems not to have impressed Lincoln and Stone, who presented their protest on March 3, after other weighty legislation (notably the bill to remove the state capital from Vandalia to Springfield) had been safely passed. (*Collected Works,* I, pp. 75n–76n.)

2

To Mary Speed [1]

Bloomington, Illinois
September 27, 1841

Miss Mary Speed,
Louisville, Ky.
 My Friend:
  . . . I assume that you have not heard from Joshua & myself since we left, because I think it doubtful whether he has written.

You remember there was some uneasiness about Joshua's health when we left. That little indisposition of his turned out to be nothing serious; and it was pretty nearly forgotten when we reached Springfield. We got on board the Steam Boat Lebanon, in the locks of the Canal about 12. o'clock. M. of the day we left, and reached St. Louis the next monday at 8 P.M. Nothing of interest happened during the passage, except the vexatious delays occasioned by the sand bars be thought interesting. By the way, a fine example was presented on board the boat for contemplating the effect of *condition* upon human happiness. A gentleman had purchased twelve negroes in different parts of Kentucky and was taking them to a farm in the South. They were chained six and six together. A small iron clevis was around the left wrist of each, and this fastened to the main chain by a shorter one at a convenient distance from, the others; so that the negroes were strung together precisely like so many fish upon a trot-line. In this condition they were being separated forever from the scenes of their childhood, their friends, their fathers and mothers, and brothers and sisters, and many of them, from their wives and children, and going into perpetual slavery where the lash of the master is proverbially more ruthless and unrelenting than any other where; and yet amid all

---

[1] Signed autograph letter, Library of Congress, Washington, D. C., in *Collected Works,* I, pp. 259–260. Mary Speed was the half-sister of Lincoln's close friend, Joshua Speed.

---

these distressing circumstances, as we would think them, they were the most cheerful and apparantly happy creatures on board. One, whose offence for which he had been sold was an over-fondness for his wife, played the fiddle almost continually; and the others danced, sung, cracked jokes, and played various games with cards from day to day. How true it is that "God tempers the wind to the shorn lamb," or in other words, that He renders the worst of human conditions tolerable, while He permits the best, to be nothing better than tolerable.

.   .   .   .   .

. . . I shall be verry happy to receive a line from you, soon after you receive this; and, in case you choose to favour me with one, address it to Charleston, Coles Co. Ills as I shall be there about the time to receive it. Your sincere friend   A. LINCOLN

3

To Williamson Durley[1]

Springfield
October 3, 1845

Friend Durley:
When I saw you at home, it was agreed that I should write to you and your brother Madison. Until I then saw you, I was not aware of your being what is generally called an abolitionist, or, as you call yourself, a Liberty-man; though I well knew there were many such in your county. I was glad to hear you say that you intend to attempt to

---

[1] Signed autograph letter, Illinois State Historical Library, Springfield, Ill., in *Collected Works,* I, pp. 347–348.

bring about, at the next election in Putnam, a union of the whigs proper, and such of the liberty men, as are whigs in principle on all questions save only that of slavery. So far as I can perceive, by such union, neither party need yield any thing, on *the* point in difference between them. If the whig abolitionists of New York had voted with us last fall, Mr. Clay would now be president, whig principles in the ascendent, and Texas not annexed; whereas by the division, all that either had at stake in the contest, was lost. And, indeed, it was extremely probable, beforehand, that such would be the result. As I always understood, the Liberty-men deprecated the annexation of Texas extremely; and, this being so, why they should refuse to so cast their votes as to prevent it, even to me, seemed wonderful. What was their process of reasoning, I can only judge from what a single one of them told me. It was this: "We are not to do *evil* that *good* may come." This general proposition is doubtless correct; but did it apply? If by your votes you could have prevented the *extention,* &c. of slavery, would it not have been *good* and not *evil* so to have used your votes, even though it involved the casting of them for a slaveholder? By the *fruit* the tree is to be known. An *evil* tree can not bring forth *good* fruit. If the fruit of electing Mr. Clay would have been to prevent the extension of slavery, could the act of electing have been *evil?*

But I will not argue farther. I perhaps ought to say that individually I never was much interested in the Texas question. I never could see much good to come of annexation; inasmuch, as they were already a free republican people on our own model; on the other hand, I never could very clearly see how the annexation would augment the evil of slavery. It always seemed to me that slaves would be taken there in about equal numbers, with or without annexation. And if more *were* taken because of annexation, still there would be just so many the fewer left, where they were taken from. It is possibly true, to some extent, that with annexation, some slaves may be sent to Texas and continued in slavery, that otherwise might have been liberated. To whatever extent this may be true, I think annexation an evil. I hold it to be a paramount duty of us in the free states, due to the Union of the states, and perhaps to liberty itself (paradox though it may seem) to let the slavery of the other states alone; while, on the other hand, I hold it to be equally clear, that we should never knowingly lend ourselves directly or indirectly, to prevent that slavery from dying a natural death—to find new places for it to live in, when it can no longer exist in the old. Of course I am not now considering what would be our duty, in cases of insurrection among the slaves.

To recur to the Texas question, I understand the Liberty men to have viewed annexation as a much greater evil than I ever did; and I would like to convince you if I could, that they could have prevented it, without violation of principle, if they had chosen.

I intend this letter for you and Madison together; and if you and he or either shall think fit to drop me a line, I shall be pleased. Yours with respect   A. LINCOLN

4

Lincoln and the Matson Negroes[1]

1847

[This 1847 case developed as follows: Anthony Bryant, a free Negro who worked for Robert Matson, found that Matson was planning to send Bryant's family to Kentucky as slaves. Matson claimed that since Mrs. Bryant and her children were only temporary visitors to Illinois, they were still legally slaves. Bryant solicited the aid of two abolitionists, Dr. Hiram Rutherford and Gideon Ashmore. Many years later, Jesse Weik, a Lincoln biographer, recorded the story as told by Dr. Rutherford, the only participant in the case who was still alive.]

Ashmore and I, having espoused the cause of the slaves, now fell under the shadow of Matson's wrath. His revenge culminated in a suit brought against us in the circuit court under the Black Law, demanding damages in the sum of twenty-five hundred dollars, or five hundred dollars for each slave. As soon as the summons was served on me I

---

[1] Jesse W. Weik, "Lincoln and the Matson Negroes: A Vista into the Fugitive Slave Days," *The Arena* (April 1897), pp. 755, 757.

rode down to Charleston to hire a lawyer. I had known Abraham Lincoln several years, and his views and mine on the wrong of slavery being in perfect accord, I determined to employ him; besides, everyone whom I consulted advised me to do so. I found him at the tavern sitting on the veranda, his chair tilted back against one of the wooden pillars, entertaining the bystanders and loungers gathered about the place with one of his irresistible and highly-flavored stories. My head was full of the impending lawsuit, and I found it a great test of my patience to await the end of the chapter then in process of narration. Before he could begin on another I interrupted and called him aside. I told in detail the story of my troubles, reminded him that we had always agreed on the questions of the day, and asked him to represent me at the trial of my case in court. He listened attentively as I recited the facts leading up to the controversy with Matson, but I noticed a peculiarly troubled look came over his face now and then, his eyes appeared to be fixed in the distance beyond me, and he shook his head several times as if debating with himself some question of grave import. At length, and with apparent reluctance, he answered that he could not defend me, because he had already been counselled with in Matson's interest, and was therefore under professional obligations to represent the latter unless released. This was a grievous disappointment, and irritated me into expressions more or less bitter in tone. He seemed to feel this, and even though he endeavored in his plausible way to reconcile me to the proposition that, as a lawyer, he must represent and be faithful to those who counsel with and employ him, I appeared not to be convinced. I remember retorting that "my money was as good an any one's else," and although thoroughly in earnest I presume I was a little too hasty.

The interview and my quick temper, I am sure, made a deep impression on Mr. Lincoln, because, a few hours latter, he despatched a messenger to me with the information that he had sent for the man who had approached him in Matson's behalf, and if they came to no more decisive terms than at first he would probably be able to represent me. In a very brief time this was followed by another message, that he could now easily and consistently free himself from Matson, and was, therefore, in a position, if I employed him, to conduct my defence. But it was too late; my pride was up, and I plainly indicated a disinclination to avail myself of his offer. Instead, I employed Charles H. Constable, a lawyer who had emigrated to Illinois from Maryland, a classical scholar, fluent and ready in debate, and of commanding physical presence. Ashmore made terms with Orlando B.

Ficklin, a Kentuckian who had already won considerable renown as a lawyer, and had been more or less conspicuous in politics.

[Lincoln represented Matson in both a proceeding in habeas corpus (brought by Rutherford and Ashmore) and in Matson's damage suit against the abolitionists. He lost both cases. Rutherford's account concludes as follows:]

. . . after the trial, which ended Saturday night, Matson left the country, crossed that Wabash river on his way to Kentucky, evaded his creditors, and *never paid Lincoln his fee*.[2]

---

[2] Six years earlier, in the case Bailey *v.* Cromwell, Lincoln had been successful in winning the freedom of a Negro girl whose owner claimed her as a slave.

5

Remarks and Resolution Introduced in the United States House of Representatives Concerning Abolition of Slavery in the District of Columbia [1]

January 10, 1849

Mr. LINCOLN said, that by the courtesy of his colleague, he would say, that if the vote on the resolution was reconsidered, he should make an effort to introduce an amendment, which he should now read.

---

[1] *Congressional Globe,* Thirtieth Congress, Second Session, p. 212. The editors of the *Collected Works* have corrected this version by comparing it to an autograph draft in the Robert Todd Lincoln Collection of the Papers of Abraham Lincoln in the Library of Congress. *Collected Works,* II, pp. 20–22.

And Mr. L. read as follows:

Strike out all before and after the word "Resolved" and insert the following, towit: That the Committee on the District of Columbia be instructed to report a bill in substance as follows, towit:

Section 1. Be it enacted by the Senate and House of Representatives of the United States of America, in Congress assembled: That no person not now within the District of Columbia, nor now owned by any person or persons now resident within it, nor hereafter born within it, shall ever be held in slavery within said District.

Section 2. That no person now within said District, or now owned by any person, or persons now resident within the same, or hereafter born within it, shall ever be held in slavery without the limits of said District: *Provided,* that officers of the government of the United States, being citizens of the slave-holding states, coming into said District on public business, and remaining only so long as may be reasonably necessary for that object, may be attended into, and out of, said District, and while there, by the necessary servants of themselves and their families, without their right to hold such servants in service, being thereby impaired.

Section 3. That all children born of slave mothers within said District on, or after the first day of January in the year of our Lord one thousand, eight hundred and fifty shall be free; but shall be reasonably supported and educated, by the respective owners of their mothers or by their heirs or representatives, and shall owe reasonable service, as apprentices, to such owners, heirs and representatives until they respectively arrive at the age of ——— years when they shall be entirely free; and the municipal authorities of Washington and Georgetown, within their respective jurisdictional limits, are hereby empowered and required to make all suitable and necessary provisions for enforcing obedience to this section, on the part of both masters and apprentices.

Section 4. That all persons now within said District lawfully held as slaves, or now owned by any person or persons now resident within said District, shall remain such, at the will of their respective owners, their heirs and legal representatives: *Provided* that any such owner, or his legal representative, may at any time receive from the treasury of the United States the full value of his or her slave, of the class in this section mentioned, upon which such slave shall be forthwith and forever free: and *provided further* that the President of the United States, the Secretary of State, and the Secretary of the Treasury shall be a board for determining the value of such slaves as their owners may desire to emancipate under this section; and whose duty it shall be to hold a session for the purpose, on the first monday of each calendar month; to receive all applications; and, on satisfactory evidence in each case, that the person presented for valuation, is a slave, and of the class in this section mentioned, and is owned by the applicant, shall value such slave at his or her full cash value, and give to the applicant an order on the treasury for the amount; and also to such slave a certificate of freedom.

Section 5. That the municipal authorities of Washington and Georgetown, within their respective jurisdictional limits, are hereby empowered and required to provide active and efficient means to arrest, and deliver up to their owners, all fugitive slaves escaping into said District.

Section 6. That the election officers within said District of Columbia, are hereby empowered and required to open polls at all the usual places of holding elections, on the first monday of April next, and receive the vote of every free white male citizen above the age of twentyone years, having resided within said District for the period of one year or more next preceding the time of such voting, for, or against this act; to proceed, in taking said votes, in all respects not herein specified, as at elections under the municipal laws; and, with as little delay as possible, to transmit correct statements of the votes so cast to the President of the United States. And it shall be the duty of the President to canvass said votes immediately, and, if a majority of them be found to be for this act, to forthwith issue his proclamation giving notice of the fact; and this act shall only be in full force and effect on, and after the day of such proclamation.

Section 7. That involuntary servitude for the punishment of crime, whereof the party shall have been duly convicted shall in no wise be prohibited by this act.

Section 8. That for all the purposes of this act the jurisdictional limits of Washington are extended to all parts of the District of Columbia not now included within the present limits of Georgetown.

Mr. LINCOLN then said, that he was authorized to say, that of about fifteen of the leading citizens of the District of Columbia to whom this proposition had been submitted, there was not one but who approved of the adoption of such a proposition. He did not wish to be misunderstood. He did not know whether or not they would vote for this bill on the first Monday of April; but he repeated, that out of fifteen persons to whom it had been submitted, he had authority to say that every one of them desired that some proposition like this should pass.[2]

---

[2] Three days later, on January 13, Lincoln gave notice of his intention to introduce the bill himself, his earlier effort having come to nothing. He never followed the announcement, however, and the document in the Lincoln Papers is doubtless the actual copy made for that purpose. Years later, in 1861, Lincoln explained that upon "finding that I was abandoned by my former backers and having little personal influence, I *dropped* the matter knowing that it was useless to prosecute the business at that time." (*Collected Works,* II, p. 22n.)

TWO

The Sectional Crisis (1854–1860)

After his brief (and undistinguished) term in Congress, Lincoln, denied political preferment by the leaders of the Whig Party, concentrated on his law practice. Thus Lincoln was on the sidelines as the great national crisis of the 1850s unfolded. As a strong admirer of Henry Clay, Lincoln supported the Compromise of 1850 as a statesmanlike way of dealing with the question of whether the new territories acquired in the Mexican war should be permitted to have slavery.

Although the compromise ended the immediate threat of disunion, the Whig Party found itself torn and divided. The breakup of the party was completed in 1854 when Stephen A. Douglas' Kansas–Nebraska Act repealed the Missouri Compromise. By permitting slavery north of the Missouri Compromise line, the Kansas–Nebraska Act seemed to many northerners—Democrats as well as Whigs—as part of an aggressive plan to spread slavery. Anti-Nebraska Democrats and Whigs came together in the new Republican Party, which included men who were united on the principle of preventing the further spread of slavery in the territories. Although Republicans opposed the expansion of slavery, they were in no sense an abolition party; they were, for the most part, opposed to Negro equality, and had no intention of disturbing slavery in those states where it already existed.

Lincoln strongly disapproved of the repeal of the Missouri Compromise and, after some hesitation, he joined the new party. In this way, Lincoln found himself in the middle of the decade with both an important political issue and a new political party that would accept him as a leader. By 1858 he was the party's candidate for Stephen A. Douglas' Senate seat; two years later he was the Republican's choice for President.

6

. . . . .

I think, and shall try to show, that it [the repeal of the Missouri Compromise] is wrong; wrong in its direct effect, letting slavery into Kansas and Nebraska—and wrong in its prospective principle, allowing it to spread to every other part of the wide world, where men can be found inclined to take it.

This *declared* indifference, but as I must think, covert *real* zeal for the spread of slavery, I can not but hate. I hate it because of the monstrous injustice of slavery itself. I hate it because it deprives our republican example of its just influence in the world—enables the enemies of free institutions, with plausibility, to taunt us as hypocrites—causes the real friends of freedom to doubt our sincerity, and especially because it forces so many really good men amongst ourselves into an open war with the very fundamental principles of civil liberty—criticising the Declaration of Independence, and insisting that there is no right principle of action but *self-interest*.

Before proceeding, let me say I think I have no prejudice against the Southern people. They are just what we would be in their situation. If slavery did not now exist amongst them, they would not introduce it. If it did now exist amongst us, we should not instantly give it up. This I believe of the masses north and south. Doubtless there are individuals, on both sides, who would not hold slaves under any circumstances; and others who would gladly introduce slavery anew, if it were out of existence. We know that some southern men do free their slaves, go north, and become tip-top abolitionists; while some northern ones go south, and become most cruel slave-masters.

When southern people tell us they are no more responsible for

---

[1] *Illinois Journal,* October 21, 23, 24, 25, 26, 27, 28, 1854, in *Collected Works,* II, pp. 255–256, 263–266, 268–271, 274–276.

the origin of slavery, than we; I acknowledge the fact. When it is said that the institution exists; and that it is very difficult to get rid of it, in any satisfactory way, I can understand and appreciate the saying. I surely will not blame them for not doing what I should not know how to do myself. If all earthly power were given me, I should not know what to do, as to the existing institution. My first impulse would be to free all the slaves, and send them to Liberia,—to their own native land. But a moment's reflection would convince me, that whatever of high hope, (as I think there is) there may be in this, in the long run, its sudden execution is impossible. If they were all landed there in a day, they would all perish in the next ten days; and there are not surplus shipping and surplus money enough in the world to carry them there in many times ten days. What then? Free them all, and keep them among us as underlings? Is it quite certain that this betters their condition? I think I would not hold one in slavery, at any rate; yet the point is not clear enough for me to denounce people upon. What next? Free them, and make them politically and socially, our equals? My own feelings will not admit of this; and if mine would, we well know that those of the great mass of white people will not. Whether this feeling accords with justice and sound judgment, is not the sole question, if indeed, it is any part of it. A universal feeling, whether well or ill-founded, can not be safely disregarded. We can not, then, make them equals. It does seem to me that systems of gradual emancipation might be adopted; but for their tardiness in this, I will not undertake to judge our brethren of the south.

When they remind us of their constitutional rights, I acknowledge them, not grudgingly, but fully, and fairly; and I would give them any legislation for the reclaiming of their fugitives, which should not, in its stringency, be more likely to carry a free man into slavery, than our ordinary criminal laws are to hang an innocent one.

But all this; to my judgment, furnishes no more excuse for permitting slavery to go into our own free territory, than it would for reviving the African slave trade by law. The law which forbids the bringing of slaves *from* Africa; and that which has so long forbid the taking them *to* Nebraska, can hardly be distinguished on any moral principle; and the repeal of the former could find quite as plausible excuses as that of the latter.

.   .   .   .   .

Another LULLABY argument is, that taking slaves to new countries does not increase their number—does not make any one slave who otherwise would be free. There is some truth in this, and I am glad of it, but it [is] not WHOLLY true. The African slave trade is not yet effectually suppressed; and if we make a reasonable deduction for the white people amongst us, who are foreigners, and the descendants of foreigners, arriving here since 1808, we shall find the increase of the black population out-running that of the white, to an extent unaccountable, except by supposing that some of them too, have been coming from Africa. If this be so, the opening of new countries to the institution, increases the demand for, and augments the price of slaves, and so does, in fact, make slaves of freemen by causing them to be brought from Africa, and sold into bondage.

But, however this may be, we know the opening of new countries to slavery, tends to the perpetuation of the institution, and so does KEEP men in slavery who otherwise would be free. This result we do not FEEL like favoring, and we are under no legal obligation to suppress our feelings in this respect.

Equal justice to the south, it is said, requires us to consent to the extending of slavery to new countries. That is to say, inasmuch as you do not object to my taking my hog to Nebraska, therefore I must not object to you taking your slave. Now, I admit this is perfectly logical, if there is no difference between hogs and negroes. . . .

. . . . . .

But one great argument in the support of the repeal of the Missouri Compromise, is still to come. That argument is "the sacred right of self government." It seems our distinguished Senator has found great difficulty in getting his antagonists, even in the Senate to meet him fairly on this argument—some poet has said

"Fools rush in where angels fear to tread."

At the hazzard of being thought one of the fools of this quotation, I meet that argument—I rush in, I take that bull by the horns.

I trust I understand, and truly estimate the right of self-government. My faith in the proposition that each man should do precisely as he pleases with all which is exclusively his own, lies at the foundation of the sense of justice there is in me. I extend the principles to communities of men, as well as to individuals. I so extend it, because it is politically wise, as well as naturally just: politically wise, in saving us from broils about matters which do not concern us. Here, or at Washington, I would not trouble myself with the oyster laws of Virginia, or the cranberry laws of Indiana.

The doctrine of self government is right—absolutely and eternally right—but it has no just application, as here attempted. Or perhaps I should rather say that whether it has such just application depends upon whether a negro is *not* or *is* a man. If he is *not* a man, why in that case, he who *is* a man may, as a matter of self-government, do just as he pleases with him. But if the negro *is* a man, is it not to that extent, a total destruction of self-government, to say that he too shall not govern *himself?* When the white man governs himself that is self-government; but when he governs himself, and also governs *another* man, that is *more* than self-government—that is despotism. If the negro is a *man,* why then my ancient faith teaches me that "all men are created equal;" and that there can be no moral right in connection with one man's making a slave of another.

Judge Douglas frequently, with bitter irony and sarcasm, paraphrases our argument by saying "The white people of Nebraska are good enough to govern themselves, *but they are not good enough to govern a few miserable negroes!!"*

Well I doubt not that the people of Nebraska are, and will continue to be as good as the average of people elsewhere. I do not say the contrary. What I do say is, that no man is good enough to govern another man, *without that other's consent.* I say this is the leading principle—the sheet anchor of American republicanism. Our Declaration of Independence says:

"We hold these truths to be self evident: that all men are created equal; that they are endowed by their Creator with certain inalienable rights; that among these are life, liberty and the pursuit of happiness. That to secure these rights, governments are instituted among men, DERIVING THEIR JUST POWERS FROM THE CONSENT OF THE GOVERNED."

I have quoted so much at this time merely to show that according to our ancient faith, the just powers of governments are derived from the consent of the governed. Now the relation of masters and slaves is, PRO TANTO, a total violation of this principle. The master not only governs the slave without his consent; but he governs him by a set of rules altogether different from those which he prescribes for himself. Allow ALL the governed an equal voice in the government, and that, and that only is self government.

Let it not be said I am contending for the establishment of political and social equality between the whites and blacks. I have already said the contrary. I am not now combating the argument of NECESSITY, arising from the fact that the blacks are already amongst us; but I am combating what is set up as MORAL argument for allowing them to be taken where they have never yet been—arguing against the EXTENSION of a bad thing, which where it already exists, we must of necessity, manage as we best can.

.   .   .   .   .

Whether slavery shall go into Nebraska, or other new territories, is not a matter of exclusive concern to the people who may go there. The whole nation is interested that the best use shall be made of these territories. We want them for the homes of free white people. This they cannot be, to any considerable extent, if slavery shall be planted within them. Slave States are places for poor white people to remove FROM; not to remove TO. New free States are the places for poor people to go to and better their condition. For this use, the nation needs these territories.

Still further; there are constitutional relations between the slave and free States, which are degrading to the latter. We are under legal obligations to catch and return their runaway slaves to them—a sort of dirty, disagreeable job, which I believe, as a general rule the slaveholders will not perform for one another. Then again, in the control of the government—the management of the partnership affairs—they have greatly the advantage of us. By the constitution, each State has two Senators—each has a number of Representatives; in proportion to the number of its people—and each has a number of presidential electors, equal to the whole number of its Senators and Representatives together. But in ascertaining the number of the people, for this purpose, five slaves are counted as being equal to three whites. The slaves do not vote; they are only counted and so used, as to swell the influence of the white people's votes. . . .

Now all this is manifestly unfair; yet I do not mention it to complain of it, in so far as it is already settled. It is in the constitution; and I do not, for that cause, or any other cause, propose to destroy, or alter, or disregard the constitution. I stand to it, fairly, fully, and firmly.

But when I am told I must leave it altogether to OTHER PEOPLE to say whether new partners are to be bred up and brought into the firm, on the same degrading terms against me, I respectfully demur. I insist, that whether I shall be a whole man, or only, the half of one, in comparison with others, is a question in which I am somewhat concerned; and one which no other man can have a sacred right of deciding for me. . . .

.   .   .   .   .

But Nebraska is urged as a great Union-saving measure. Well I too, go for saving the Union. Much as I hate slavery, I would consent to the extension of it rather than see the Union dissolved, just as I would consent to any GREAT evil, to avoid a GREATER one. But when I go to Union saving, I must believe, at least, that the means I employ has some adaptation to the end. To my mind, Nebraska has no such adaptation.

"It hath no relish of salvation in it."

It is an aggravation, rather, of the only one thing which ever endangers the Union. When it came upon us, all was peace and quiet. The nation was looking to the forming of new bonds of Union; and a long course of peace and prosperity seemed to lie before us. In the whole range of possibility, there scarcely appears to me to have been any thing, out of which the slavery agitation could have been revived, except the very project of repealing the Missouri compromise. Every inch of territory we owned, already had a definite settlement of the slavery question, and by which, all parties were pledged to abide. Indeed, there was no uninhabited country on the continent, which we could acquire; if we except some extreme northern regions, which are wholly out of the question. In this state of case, the genius of Discord himself, could scarcely have invented a way of again getting [setting?] us by the ears, but by turning back and destroying the peace measures of the past. The councils of that genius seem to have prevailed, the Missouri compromise was repealed; and here we are, in the midst of a new slavery agitation, such, I think, as we have never seen before. Who is responsible for this? Is it those who resist the measure; or those who, causelessly, brought it forward, and pressed it through, having reason to know, and, in fact, knowing it must and would be so resisted? It could not but be expected by its author, that it would be looked upon as a measure for the extension of slavery, aggravated by a gross breach of faith. Argue as you will, and long as you will, this is the naked FRONT and ASPECT, of the measure. And in this aspect, it could not but produce agitation. Slavery is founded in the selfishness of man's nature—opposition to it, is [in?] his love of justice. These principles are an eternal antagonism; and when brought into collision so fiercely, as slavery extension brings them, shocks, and throes, and convulsions must ceaselessly follow. Repeal the Missouri compromise —repeal all compromises—repeal the declaration of independence— repeal all past history, you still can not repeal human nature. It still will be the abundance of man's heart, that slavery extension is wrong; and out of the abundance of his heart, his mouth will continue to speak.

.   .   .   .   .

I particularly object to the NEW position which the avowed principle of this Nebraska law gives to slavery in the body politic. I object to it because it assumes that there CAN be MORAL RIGHT in the enslaving of one man by another. I object to it as a dangerous dalliance for a few [free?] people—a sad evidence that, feeling prosperity we forget right—that liberty, as a principle, we have ceased to revere. I object to it because the fathers of the republic eschewed, and rejected it. The argument of "Necessity" was the only argument they ever admitted in favor of slavery; and so far, and so far only as it carried them, did they ever go. They found the institution existing among us, which they could not help; and they cast blame upon the British King for having permitted its introduction. BEFORE the constitution, they prohibited its introduction into the north-western Territory—the only country we owned, then free from it. AT the framing and adoption of the constitution, they forbore to so much as mention the word "slave" or "slavery" in the whole instrument. In the provision for the recovery of fugitives, the slave is spoken of as a "PERSON HELD TO SERVICE OR LABOR." In that prohibiting the abolition of the African slave trade for twenty years, that trade is spoken of as "The migration or importation of such persons as any of the States NOW EXISTING, shall think proper to admit," &c. These are the only provisions alluding to slavery. Thus, the thing is hid away, in the constitution, just as an afflicted man hides away a wen or a cancer, which he dares not cut out at once, lest he bleed to death; with the promise, nevertheless, that the cutting may begin at the end of a given time. Less than this our fathers COULD not do; and NOW [MORE?] they WOULD not do. Necessity drove them so far, and farther, they would not go. But this is not all. The earliest Congress, under the constitution, took the same view of slavery. They hedged and hemmed it in to the narrowest limits of necessity.

.   .   .   .   .

But NOW it is to be transformed into a "sacred right." Nebraska brings it forth, places it on the high road to extension and perpetuity; and, with a pat on its back, says to it, "Go, and God speed you." Henceforth it is to be the chief jewel of the nation—the very figure-head of the ship of State. Little by little, but steadily as man's march to the grave, we have been giving up the OLD for the NEW faith. Near eighty years ago we began by declaring that all men are created equal; but now from that beginning we have run down to the other declaration, that for SOME men to enslave OTHERS is a "sacred right of self-government." These principles can not stand together. They are as opposite as God and mammon; and whoever holds to the one, must despise the other. When Pettit, in connection with his support of the Nebraska bill, called the Declaration of Independence "a self-evident lie" he only did what consistency and candor require all other Nebraska men to do. Of the forty odd Nebraska Senators who sat present and heard him, no one rebuked him. Nor am I apprized that any Nebraska newspaper, or any Nebraska orator, in the whole nation, has ever yet rebuked him. If this had been among Marion's men, Southerners though they were, what would have become of the man who said it? If this had been said to the men who captured André, the man who said it, would probably have been hung sooner than André was. If it had been said in old Independence Hall, seventy-eight years ago, the very door-keeper would have throttled the man, and thrust him into the street.

Let no one be deceived. The spirit of seventy-six and the spirit of Nebraska, are utter antagonisms; and the former is being rapidly displaced by the latter.

Fellow countrymen—Americans south, as well as north, shall we make no effort to arrest this? Already the liberal party throughout the world, express the apprehension "that the one retrograde institution in America, is undermining the principles of progress, and fatally violating the noblest political system the world ever saw." This is not the taunt of enemies, but the warning of friends. Is it quite safe to disregard it—to despise it? Is there no danger to liberty itself, in discarding the earliest practice, and first precept of our ancient faith? In our greedy chase to make profit of the negro, let us beware, lest we "cancel and tear to pieces" even the white man's charter of freedom.

Our republican robe is soiled, and trailed in the dust. Let us re-purify it. Let us turn and wash it white, in the spirit, if not the blood, of the Revolution. Let us turn slavery from its claims of "moral right," back upon its existing legal rights, and its arguments of "necessity." Let us return it to the position our fathers gave it; and there let it rest in peace. Let us re-adopt the Declaration of Independence, and with it, the practices, and policy, which harmonize with it. Let north and south—let all Americans—let all lovers of liberty everywhere—join in the great and good work. If we do this, we shall not only have saved the Union; but we shall have so saved it, as to make, and to keep it, forever worthy of the saving. We shall have so saved it, that the succeeding millions of free happy people, the world over, shall rise up, and call us blessed, to the latest generations.

. . . . .

7

Henry A. Groves to Abraham Lincoln[1]

Peoria
November 18, 1854

Dear Sir

Your favor of 13th inst is now before me. Absence from home on a visit to Chicago prevented an earlier answer.

---

[1] Robert Todd Lincoln Collection, Library of Congress, in David C. Mearns, *The Lincoln Papers: The Story of the Collection with Selections to July 4, 1861*, 2 vols. (Garden City, N. Y.: Doubleday & Co., 1948), I, pp. 195–196. Grove was a Whig member of the Illinois House of Representatives.

I have no objection to stating fully my views as to the United States Senatorship. I believe that a very large majority of the men who voted for me expect me to vote for you, that is they prefer you to any other person. I confess also that so far as I am acquainted with your political views I prefer you to any other person, but before committing myself fully, it would afford me pleasure to hear from you as to one or two matters further.

1. Are you eligible to the office under our constitution. My information is that you are a member elect to the House.

2. I understand you to be opposed to the extension of Slavery into Territory now free: I would expect you to maintain this position on all occasions.

3. At some time when it could be done in a proper spirit I should like to see Slavery abolished in the District of Columbia. In my judgment the continuance of Slavery there works no benefit to the institution in the States. I disclaim all right on the part of the Federal Government to interfere with the institution of Slavery when it exists in the States, but the power of the Government over the District is allmost universally conceded and in a proper time & manner I would rejoice to see it abolished there. Would you vote for such a law. I don't ask to become an agitator nor to go for it as a matter of insult or invitation to the South but in your own quiet good humoured way relieve the nation of the disgrace of sanctioning slavery at the National capital. And if you cannot go for that would you go for submitting the question to the people of that District for settlement. If your views harmonize with mine then you are my man as at present admired. As to your views on national policy they accord with my own altogether. You may put me down as pretty sure for Abe. Will you do me the favor to send me a copy of the rules of the last House. Who do you go for for Speaker. Do you know just how matters will stand with us so far as the two houses are concerned

Yours truly
H. Grove

Hon A. Lincoln

P.S. One word further I dont want you to commit yourself to any party or views. Think and act as becomes the Senator of Illinois & Lincoln, but dont lash us to Slavery in any way.[2]

---

[2] Neither Lincoln's original letter to Grove nor his reply to this letter have been found; Lincoln wrote several letters asking for support in his bid for the Senate.

8

To George Robertson[1]

Springfield, Illinois
August 15, 1855

Hon: Geo. Robertson
Lexington, Ky.

My dear Sir: The volume you left for me has been received. I am really grateful for the honor of your kind remembrance, as well as for the book. The partial reading I have already given it, has afforded me much of both pleasure and instruction. It was new to me that the exact question which led to the Missouri compromise, had arisen before it arose in regard to Missouri; and that you had taken so prominent a part in it. Your short, but able and patriotic speech upon that occasion, has not been improved upon since, by those holding the same views; and, with all the lights you then had, the views you took appear to me as very reasonable.

You are not a friend of slavery in the abstract. In that speech you spoke of *"the peaceful extinction of slavery"* and used other expressions indicating your belief that the thing was, at some time, to have an end[.] Since then we have had thirty six years of experience; and this experience has demonstrated, I think, that there is no peaceful extinction of slavery in prospect for us. The signal failure of Henry Clay, and other good and great men, in 1849, to effect any thing in favor of gradual emancipation in Kentucky, together with a thousand other signs, extinguishes that hope utterly. On the question of liberty, as a principle, we are not what we have been. When we were the political slaves of King George, and wanted to be free, we called the maxim that "all men are created equal" a self evident truth; but now when we have grown fat, and have lost all dread of being slaves ourselves, we have become so greedy to be *masters* that we call the same

---

[1] Signed autograph letter, Library of Congress, in *Collected Works,* II, pp. 317–318.

---

maxim "a self-evident lie." The fourth of July has not quite dwindled away; it is still a great day—*for burning fire-crackers!!!*

That spirit which desired the peaceful extinction of slavery, has itself become extinct, with the *occasion,* and the *men* of the Revolution. Under the impulse of that occasion, nearly half the states adopted systems of emancipation at once; and it is a significant fact, that not a single state has done the like since. So far as peaceful, voluntary emancipation is concerned, the condition of the negro slave in America, scarcely less terrible to the contemplation of a free mind, is now as fixed, and hopeless of change for the better, as that of the lost souls of the finally impenitent. The Autocrat of all the Russias will resign his crown, and proclaim his subjects free republicans sooner than will our American masters voluntarily give up their slaves.

Our political problem now is "Can we, as a nation, continue together *permanently—forever—*half slave, and half free?" The problem is too mighty for me. May God, in his mercy, superintend the solution. Your much obliged friend, and humble servant

A. LINCOLN

9

To Joshua F. Speed [1]

Springfield
August 24, 1855

Dear Speed:

You know what a poor correspondent I am. Ever since I received your very agreeable letter of the 22nd. of May I have been intending to write you in answer to it. You suggest that in political action

---

[1] Signed autograph letter, Massachusetts Historical Society, Boston, Mass., in *Collected Works,* II, pp. 320, 322–323.

---

now, you and I would differ. I suppose we would; not quite as much, however, as you may think. You know I dislike slavery; and you fully admit the abstract wrong of it. So far there is no cause of difference. But you say that sooner than yield your legal right to the slave— especially at the bidding of those who are not themselves interested, you would see the Union dissolved. I am not aware that *any one* is bidding you to yield that right; very certainly *I* am not. I leave that matter entirely to yourself. I also acknowledge *your* rights and *my* obligations, under the constitution, in regard to your slaves. I confess I hate to see the poor creatures hunted down, and caught, and carried back to their stripes, and unrewarded toils; but I bite my lip and keep quiet. In 1841 you and I had together a tedious low-water trip, on a Steam Boat from Louisville to St. Louis. You may remember, as I well do, that from Louisville to the mouth of the Ohio there were, on board, ten or a dozen slaves, shackled together with irons. That sight was a continual torment to me; and I see something like it every time I touch the Ohio, or any other slave-border. It is hardly fair for you to assume, that I have no interest in a thing which has, and continually exercises, the power of making me miserable. You ought rather to appreciate how much the great body of the Northern people do crucify their feelings, in order to maintain their loyalty to the constitution and the Union.

I do oppose the extension of slavery, because my judgment and feelings so prompt me; and I am under no obligation to the contrary. If for this you and I must differ, differ we must. . . .

.   .   .   .   .

You say if Kansas fairly votes herself a free state, as a christian you will rather rejoice at it. All decent slave-holders *talk* that way; and I do not doubt their candor. But they never *vote* that way. Although in a private letter, or conversation, you will express your preference that Kansas shall be free, you would vote for no man for Congress who would say the same thing publicly. No such man could be elected from any district in any slave-state. You think Stringfellow & Co ought to be hung; and yet, at the next presidential election you will vote for the exact type and representative of Stringfellow. The slave-breeders and slave-traders, are a small, odious and detested class, among you; and yet in politics, they dictate the course of all of you, and are as completely your masters, as you are the masters of your own negroes.

You enquire where I now stand. That is a disputed point. I think I am a whig; but others say there are no whigs, and that I am an abolitionist. When I was at Washington I voted for the Wilmot Proviso as good as forty times, and I never heard of any one attempting to unwhig me for that. I now do no more than oppose the *extension* of slavery.

I am not a Know-Nothing. That is certain. How could I be? How can any one who abhors the oppression of negroes, be in favor of degrading classes of white people? Our progress in degeneracy appears to me to be pretty rapid. As a nation, we began by declaring that *"all men are created equal."* We now practically read it "all men are created equal, *except negroes."* When the Know-Nothings get control, it will read "all men are created equal, except negroes, *and foreigners, and catholics."* When it comes to this I should prefer emigrating to some country where they make no pretence of loving liberty—to Russia, for instance, where despotism can be taken pure, and without the base alloy of hypocracy.

Mary will probably pass a day or two in Louisville in October. My kindest regards to Mrs. Speed. On the leading subject of this letter, I have more of her sympathy than I have of yours.

And yet let [me] say I am   Your friend forever

A. LINCOLN

10

Speech at Springfield, Illinois[1]

June 26, 1857

FELLOW CITIZENS:—I am here to-night, partly by the invitation of some of you and partly by my own inclination. Two weeks ago Judge Douglas spoke here on the several subjects of Kansas, the

---

[1] *Illinois State Journal,* June 29, 1857, in *Collected Works,* II, pp. 398, 403–410.

Dred Scott decision, and Utah. I listened to the speech at the time, and have read the report of it since. It was intended to controvert opinions which I think just, and to assail (politically, not personally,) those men who, in common with me, entertain those opinions. For this reason I wished then, and still wish, to make some answer to it, which I now take the opportunity of doing.

.   .   .   .   .

There is a natural disgust in the minds of nearly all white people, to the idea of an indiscriminate amalgamation of the white and black races; and Judge Douglas evidently is basing his chief hope, upon the chances of being able to appropriate the benefit of this disgust to himself. If he can, by much drumming and repeating, fasten the odium of that idea upon his adversaries, he thinks he can struggle through the storm. He therefore clings to this hope, as a drowning man to the last plank. He makes an occasion for lugging it in from the opposition to the Dred Scott decision. He finds the Republicans insisting that the Declaration of Independence includes ALL men, black as well as white; and forthwith he boldly denies that it includes negroes at all, and proceeds to argue gravely that all who contend it does, do so only because they want to vote, and eat, and sleep, and marry with negroes! He will have it that they cannot be consistent else. Now I protest against that counterfeit logic which concludes that, because I do not want a black woman for a *slave* I must necessarily want her for a *wife*. I need not have her for either, I can just leave her alone. In some respects she certainly is not my equal; but in her natural right to eat the bread she earns with her own hands without asking leave of any one else, she is my equal, and the equal of all others.

Chief Justice Taney, in his opinion in the Dred Scott case, admits that the language of the Declaration is broad enough to include the whole human family, but he and Judge Douglas argue that the authors of that instrument did not intend to include negroes, by the fact that they did not at once, actually place them on an equality with the whites. Now this grave argument comes to just nothing at all, by the other fact, that they did not at once, *or ever afterwards,* actually place all white people on an equality with one or another. And this is the staple argument of both the Chief Justice and the Senator, for doing this obvious violence to the plain unmistakable language of the Declaration. I think the authors of that notable instrument intended to include *all* men, but they did not intend to declare all men equal in *all respects*. They did not mean to say all were equal in color, size, intellect, moral developments, or social capacity. They defined with tolerable distinctness, in what respects they did consider all men created equal—equal in "certain inalienable rights, among which are life, liberty, and the pursuit of happiness." This they said, and this meant. They did not mean to assert the obvious untruth, that all were then actually enjoying that equality, nor yet, that they were about to confer it immediately upon them. In fact they had no power to confer such a boon. They meant simply to declare the *right,* so that the *enforcement* of it might follow as fast as circumstances should permit. They meant to set up a standard maxim for free society, which should be familiar to all, and revered by all; constantly looked to, constantly labored for, and even though never perfectly attained, constantly approximated, and thereby constantly spreading and deepening its influence, and augmenting the happiness and value of life to all people of all colors everywhere. The assertion that "all men are created equal" was of no practical use in effecting our separation from Great Britain; and it was placed in the Declaration, not for that, but for future use. Its authors meant it to be, thank God, it is now proving itself, a stumbling block to those who in after times might seek to turn a free people back into the hateful paths of despotism. They knew the proneness of prosperity to breed tyrants, and they meant when such should re-appear in this fair land and commence their vocation they should find left for them at least one hard nut to crack.

.   .   .   .   .

But Judge Douglas is especially horrified at the thought of the mixing blood by the white and black races: agreed for once—a thousand times agreed. There are white men enough to marry all the white women, and black men enough to marry all the black women; and so let them be married. On this point we fully agree with the Judge; and when he shall show that his policy is better adapted to prevent amalgamation than ours we shall drop ours, and adopt his. . . .
. . . [S]tatistics show that slavery is the greatest source of amalgamation; and next to it, not the elevation, but the degeneration of the free blacks. Yet Judge Douglas dreads the slightest restraints on the spread of slavery, and the slightest human recognition of the negro, as tending horribly to amalgamation.

.   .   .   .   .

I have said that the separation of the races is the only perfect preventive of amalgamation. I have no right to say all the members of the Republican party are in favor of this, nor to say that as a party they are in favor of it. There is nothing in their platform directly on the subject. But I can say a very large proportion of its members are for it, and that the chief plank in their platform—opposition to the spread of slavery—is most favorable to that separation.

Such separation, if ever effected at all, must be effected by colonization; and no political party, as such, is now doing anything directly for colonization. Party operations at present only favor or retard colonization incidentally. The enterprise is a difficult one; but "when there is a will there is a way;" and what colonization needs most is a hearty will. Will springs from the two elements of moral sense and self-interest. Let us be brought to believe it is morally right, and, at the same time, favorable to, or, at least, not against, our interest, to transfer the African to his native clime, and we shall find a way to do it, however great the task may be. The children of Israel, to such members as to include four hundred thousand fighting men, went out of Egyptian bondage in a body.

How differently the respective courses of the Democratic and Republican parties incidentally bear on the question of forming a will —a public sentiment—for colonization, is easy to see. The Republicans inculcate, with whatever of ability they can, that the negro is a man; that his bondage is cruelly wrong, and that the field of his oppression ought not to be enlarged. The Democrats deny his manhood; deny, or dwarf to insignificance, the wrong of his bondage; so far as possible, crush all sympathy for him, and cultivate and excite hatred and disgust against him; compliment themselves as Union-savers for doing so; and call the indefinite outspreading of his bondage "a sacred right of self-government."

The plainest print cannot be read through a gold eagle; and it will be ever hard to find many men who will send a slave to Liberia, and pay his passage while they can send him to a new country, Kansas for instance, and sell him for fifteen hundred dollars, and the rise.

11

"A House Divided":
Speech at Springfield, Illinois[1]

June 16, 1858

The Speech, immediately succeeding, was delivered, June 16, 1858 at Springfield Illinois, at the close of the Republican State convention held at that time and place; and by which convention Mr. Lincoln had been named as their candidate for U. S. Senator.

Senator Douglas was not present.

Mr. PRESIDENT and Gentlemen of the Convention.

If we could first know *where* we are, and *whither* we are tending, we could then better judge *what* to do, and *how* to do it.

We are now far into the *fifth* year, since a policy was initiated, with the *avowed* object, and *confident* promise, of putting an end to slavery agitation.

Under the operation of that policy, that agitation has not only, *not ceased,* but has *constantly augmented.*

In *my* opinion, it *will* not cease, until a *crisis* shall have been reached, and passed.

"A house divided against itself cannot stand."

I believe this government cannot endure, permanently half *slave* and half *free.*

I do not expect the Union to be *dissolved*—I do not expect the house to *fall*—but I *do* expect it will cease to be divided.

It will become *all* one thing, or *all* the other.

Either the *opponents* of slavery, will arrest the further spread of it, and place it where the public mind shall rest in the belief that it is in course of ultimate extinction; or its *advocates* will push it for-

---

[1] *Illinois State Journal,* June 18, 1858. The editors of the *Collected Works* have made corrections in this text by comparing it with the text that Lincoln clipped, corrected, and mounted in his Debates Scrapbook, now in the Library of Congress. *Collected Works,* II, pp. 461–462, 464–467.

ward, till it shall become alike lawful in *all* the States, *old* as well as *new*—*North* as well as *South*.

Have we no *tendency* to the latter condition?

Let any one who doubts, carefully contemplate that now almost complete legal combination—piece of *machinery* so to speak—compounded of the Nebraska doctrine, and the Dred Scott decision. Let him consider not only *what work* the machinery is adapted to do, and *how well* adapted; but also, let him study the *history* of its construction, and trace, if he can, or rather *fail,* if he can, to trace the evidences of design, and concert of action, among its chief bosses, from the beginning.

.   .   .   .   .

The *working* points of that machinery are:

First, that no negro slave, imported as such from Africa, and no descendant of such slave can ever be a *citizen* of any State, in the sense of that term as used in the Constitution of the United States.

This point is made in order to deprive the negro, in every possible event, of the benefit of this provision of the United States Constitution, which declares that—

"The citizens of each State shall be entitled to all privileges and immunities of citizens in the several States."

Secondly, that "subject to the Constitution of the United States," neither *Congress* nor a *Territorial Legislature* can exclude slavery from any United States territory.

This point is made in order that individual men may *fill up* the territories with slaves, without danger of losing them as property, and thus to enhance the chances of *permanency* to the institution through all the future.

Thirdly, that whether the holding a negro in actual slavery in a free State, makes him free, as against the holder, the United States courts will not decide, but will leave to be decided by the courts of any slave State the negro may be forced into by the master.

This point is made, not to be pressed *immediately;* but, if acquiesced in for a while, and apparently *indorsed* by the people at an election, *then* to sustain the logical conclusion that what Dred Scott's master might lawfully do with Dred Scott, in the free State of Illinois, every other master may lawfully do with any other *one,* or one *thousand* slaves, in Illinois, or in any other free State.

Auxiliary to all this, and working hand in hand with it, the Nebraska doctrine, or what is left of it, is to *educate* and *mould* public opinion, at least *Northern* public opinion, to not *care* whether slavery is voted *down* or voted *up.*

This shows exactly where we now *are;* and *partially* also, whither we are tending.

It will throw additional light on the latter, to go back, and run the mind over the string of historical facts already stated. Several things will *now* appear less *dark* and *mysterious* than they did *when* they were transpiring. . . .

. . . . .

It should not be overlooked that, by the Nebraska bill, the people of a *State* as well as *Territory,* were to be left *"perfectly free"* *"subject only to the Constitution."*

Why mention a *State?* They were legislating for *territories,* and not *for* or *about* States. Certainly the people of a State *are* and *ought to be* subject to the Constitution of the United States; but why is mention of this *lugged* into this merely *territorial* law? Why are the people of a *territory* and the people of a *state* therein *lumped* together, and their relation to the Constitution therein treated as being *precisely* the same?

While the opinion of *the Court,* by Chief Justice Taney, in the Dred Scott case, and the separate opinions of all the concurring Judges, expressly declare that the Constitution of the United States neither permits Congress nor a Territorial legislature to exclude slavery from any United States territory, they all *omit* to declare whether or not the same Constitution permits a *state,* or the people of a State, to exclude it.

Possibly, this was a mere *omission;* but who can be *quite* sure . . .

The nearest approach to the point of declaring the power of a State over slavery, is made by Judge Nelson. He approaches it more than once, using the precise idea, and *almost* the language too, of the Nebraska act. On one occasion his exact language is, "except in cases where the power is restrained by the Constitution of the United States, the law of the State is supreme over the subject of slavery within its jurisdiction."

In what *cases* the power of the *states is* so restrained by the U.S. Constitution, is left an *open* question, precisely as the same question, as to the restraint on the power of the *territories* was left open in the Nebraska act. Put *that* and *that* together, and we have another nice little niche, which we may, ere long, see filled with another Supreme

Court decision, declaring that the Constitution of the United States does not permit a *state* to exclude slavery from its limits.

And this may especially be expected if the doctrine of "care not whether slavery be voted *down* or voted *up*," shall gain upon the public mind sufficiently to give promise that such a decision can be maintained when made.

Such a decision is all that slavery now lacks of being alike lawful in all the States.

Welcome or unwelcome, such decision *is* probably coming, and will soon be upon us, unless the power of the present political dynasty shall be met and overthrown.

We shall *lie down* pleasantly dreaming that the people of *Missouri* are on the verge of making their State *free;* and we shall *awake* to the *reality,* instead, that the *Supreme* Court has made *Illinois* a *slave* State.

To meet and overthrow the power of that dynasty, is the work now before all those who would prevent that consummation.

.   .   .   .   .

12

Speech at Chicago, Illinois[1]

July 10, 1858

.   .   .   .   .

Judge Douglas made two points upon my recent speech at Springfield. He says they are to be the issues of this campaign. The first one of these points he bases upon the language in a speech which I delivered at Springfield. . . .

---

[1] Debates Scrapbook, in *Collected Works,* II, pp. 490–494, 501.

. . . I want your attention particularly to what he has inferred from it. He says I am in favor of making all the States of this Union uniform in all their internal regulations; that in all their domestic concerns I am in favor of making them entirely uniform. He draws this inference from the language I have quoted to you. He says that I am in favor of making war by the North upon the South for the extinction of slavery; that I am also in favor of inviting (as he expresses it) the South to a war upon the North, for the purpose of nationalizing slavery. Now, it is singular enough, if you will carefully read that passage over, that I did not say that I was in favor of anything in it. I only said what I expected would take place. I made a prediction only—it may have been a foolish one perhaps. I did not even say that I desired that slavery should be put in course of ultimate extinction. I do say so now, however, [great applause] so there need be no longer any difficulty about that. It may be written down in the great [next?] speech. [Applause and laughter.]

Gentlemen, Judge Douglas informed you that this speech of mine was probably carefully prepared. I admit that it was. I am not master of language; I have not a fine education; I am not capable of entering into a disquisition upon dialectics, as I believe you call it; but I do not believe the language I employed bears any such construction as Judge Douglas put upon it. But I don't care about a quibble in regard to words. I know what I meant, and I will not leave this crowd in doubt, if I can explain it to them, what I really meant in the use of that paragraph.

I am not, in the first place, unaware that this Government has endured eighty-two years, half slave and half free. I know that. I am tolerably well acquainted with the history of the country, and I know that it has endured eighty-two years, half slave and half free. I *believe* —and that is what I meant to allude to there—I *believe* it has endured because, during all that time, until the introduction of the Nebraska Bill, the public mind did rest, all the time, in the belief that slavery was in course of ultimate extinction. ["Good!" "Good!" and applause.] That was what gave us the rest that we had through that period of eighty-two years; at least, so I believe. I have always hated slavery, I think as much as any Abolitionist. [Applause.] I have been an Old Line Whig. I have always hated it, but I have always been quiet about it until this new era of the introduction of the Nebraska Bill began. I always believed that everybody was against it, and that it was in course of ultimate extinction. (Pointing to Mr. Browning, who stood near by.) Browning thought so; the great mass of the nation have rested in the belief that slavery was in course of ultimate extinction. They had reason so to believe.

The adoption of the Constitution and its attendant history led the people to believe so; and that such was the belief of the framers of the Constitution itself. Why did those old men, about the time of the adoption of the Constitution, decree that Slavery should not go into the new Territory, where it had not already gone? Why declare that within twenty years the African Slave Trade, by which slaves are supplied, might be cut off by Congress? Why were all these acts? I might enumerate more of these acts—but enough. What were they but a clear indication that the framers of the Constitution intended and expected the ultimate extinction of that institution. [Cheers.] And now, when I say, as I said in my speech that Judge Douglas has quoted from, when I say that I think the opponents of slavery will resist the farther spread of it, and place it where the public mind shall rest with the belief that it is in course of ultimate extinction, I only mean to say, that they will place it where the founders of this Government originally placed it.

I have said a hundred times, and I have now no inclination to take it back, that I believe there is no right, and ought to be no inclination in the people of the free States to enter into the slave States, and interfere with the question of slavery at all. I have said that always. Judge Douglas has heard me say it—if not quite a hundred times, at least as good as a hundred times; and when it is said that I am in favor of interfering with slavery where it exists, I know it is unwarranted by anything I have ever *intended,* and, as I believe, by anything I have ever *said.* If, by any means, I have ever used language which could fairly be so construed, (as, however, I believe I never have,) I now correct it.

[Here the shouts of the Seventh Ward Delegation announced that they were coming in procession. They were received with enthusiastic cheers.]

So much, then, for the inference that Judge Douglas draws, that I am in favor of setting the sections at war with one another. I know that I never meant any such thing, and I believe that no fair mind can infer any such thing from anything I have ever said. ["Good," "good."]

Now in relation to his inference that I am in favor of a general consolidation of all the local institutions of the various States. I will attend to that for a little while, and try to inquire, if I can, how on earth it could be that any man could draw such an inference from anything I said. . . .

How is it, then, that Judge Douglas infers, because I hope to see slavery put where the public mind shall rest in the belief that it is in the course of ultimate extinction, that I am in favor of Illinois going over and interfering with the cranberry laws of Indiana? What can authorize him to draw any such inference? I suppose there might be one thing that at least enabled *him* to draw such an inference that would not be true with me or with many others, that is, because he looks upon all this matter of slavery as an exceedingly little thing—this matter of keeping one-sixth of the population of the whole nation in a state of oppression and tyranny unequalled in the world. He looks upon it as being an exceedingly little thing—only equal to the question of the cranberry laws of Indiana—as something having no moral question in it—as something on a par with the question of whether a man shall pasture his land with cattle, or plant it with tobacco—so little and so small a thing, that he concludes, if I could desire that anything should be done to bring about the ultimate extinction of that little thing, I must be in favor of bringing about an amalgamation of all the other little things in the Union. Now, it so happens—and there, I presume, is the foundation of this mistake—that the Judge thinks thus; and it so happens that there is a vast portion of the American people that do *not* look upon that matter as being this very little thing. They look upon it as a vast moral evil; they can prove it is such by the writings of those who gave us the blessings of liberty which we enjoy, and that they so looked upon it, and not as an evil merely confining itself to the States where it is situated; and while we agree that, by the Constitution we assented to, in the States where it exists we have no right to interfere with it because it is in the Constitution and we are by both duty and inclination to stick by that Constitution in all its letter and spirit from beginning to end. [Great applause.]

. . . . . .

Now, sirs, for the purpose of squaring things with this idea of "don't care if slavery is voted up or voted down," for sustaining the Dred Scott decision [A voice—"Hit him again"], for holding that the Declaration of Independence did not mean anything at all, we have Judge Douglas giving his exposition of what the Declaration of Independence means, and we have him saying that the people of America are equal to the people of England. According to his construction, you Germans are not connected with it. Now I ask you in all soberness, if all these things, if indulged in, if ratified, if confirmed and endorsed, if taught to our children, and repeated to them, do not tend to rub out the sentiment of liberty in the country, and to transform this Government into a government of some other form. Those arguments that are made, that the inferior race are to be treated with as much allowance as they are capable of enjoying; that as much is to be done for them as their condition will allow. What are these arguments? They are the arguments that kings have made for enslaving the people in all ages of the world. You will find that all the arguments in favor of king-craft were of this class; they always bestrode the necks of the people, not that they wanted to do it, but because the people were better off for being ridden. That is their argument, and this argument of the Judge is the same old serpent that says you work and I eat, you toil and I will enjoy the fruits of it. Turn in [it?] whatever way you will—whether it come from the mouth of a King, an excuse for enslaving the people of his country, or from the mouth of men of one race as a reason for enslaving the men of another race, it is all the same old serpent, and I hold if that course of argumentation that is made for the purpose of convincing the public mind that we should not care about this, should be granted, it does not stop with the negro. I should like to know if taking this old Declaration of Independence, which declares that all men are equal upon principle and making exceptions to it where will it stop. If one man says it does not mean a negro, why [may] not another say it does not mean some other man? If that declaration is not the truth, let us get the Statute book, in which we find it and tear it out! Who is so bold as to do it! [Voices—"me" "no one," &c.] If it is not true let us tear it out! [cries of "no, no,"] let us stick to it then, [cheers] let us stand firmly by it then. [Applause.]

It may be argued that there are certain conditions that make necessities and impose them upon us, and to the extent that a necessity is imposed upon a man he must submit to it. I think that was the condition in which we found ourselves when we established this government. We had slavery among us, we could not get our constitution unless we permitted them to remain in slavery, we could not secure the good we did secure if we grasped for more, and having by necessity submitted to that much, it does not destroy the principle that is the charter of our liberties. Let that charter stand as our standard.

My friend has said to me that I am a poor hand to quote Scripture. I will try it again, however. It is said in one of the admonitions of the Lord, "As your Father in Heaven is perfect, be ye also perfect." The Savior, I suppose, did not expect that any human creature could be perfect as the Father in Heaven; but He said, "As your Father in Heaven is perfect, be ye also perfect." He set that up as a standard, and he who did most towards reaching that standard, attained the highest degree of moral perfection. So I say in relation to the principle that all men are created equal, let it be as nearly reached as we can. If we cannot give freedom to every creature, let us do nothing that will impose slavery upon any other creature. [Applause.] Let us then turn this government back into the channel in which the framers of the Constitution originally placed it. Let us stand firmly by each other. If we do not do so we are turning in the contrary direction, that our friend Judge Douglas proposes—not intentionally—as working in the traces [that] tend to make this one universal slave nation. [A voice—"that is so."] He is one that runs in that direction, and as such I resist him.

My friends, I have detained you about as long as I desired to do, and I have only to say, let us discard all this quibbling about this man and the other man—this race and that race and the other race being inferior, and therefore they must be placed in an inferior position—discarding our standard that we have left us. Let us discard all these things, and unite as one people throughout this land, until we shall once more stand up declaring that all men are created equal.

. . . . .

13

First Debate with
Stephen A. Douglas at Ottawa, Illinois[1]

August 21, 1858

Mr. Douglas' Speech:
Ladies and gentlemen: I appear before you to-day for the purpose of discussing the leading political topics which now agitate the public mind. By an arrangement between Mr. Lincoln and myself, we

---

[1] Debates Scrapbook, in *Collected Works*, III, pp. 9–10, 16.

---

are present here to-day for the purpose of having a joint discussion as the representatives of the two great political parties of the State and Union, upon the principles in issue between these parties and this vast concourse of people, shows the deep feeling which pervades the public mind in regard to the questions dividing us.

.   .   .   .   .

We are told by Lincoln that he is utterly opposed to the Dred Scott decision, and will not submit to it, for the reason that he says it deprives the negro of the rights and privileges of citizenship. (Laughter and applause.) That is the first and main reason which he assigns for his warfare on the Supreme Court of the United States and its decision. I ask you, are you in favor of conferring upon the negro the rights and privileges of citizenship? ("No, no.") Do you desire to strike out of our State Constitution that clause which keeps slaves and free negroes out of the State, and allow the free negroes to flow in, ("never,") and cover your prairies with black settlements? Do you desire to turn this beautiful State into a free negro colony, ("no, no,") in order that when Missouri abolishes slavery she can send one hundred thousand emancipated slaves into Illinois, to become citizens and voters, on an equality with yourselves? ("Never," "no.") If you desire negro citizenship, if you desire to allow them to come into the State and settle with the white man, if you desire them to vote on an equality with yourselves, and to make them eligible to office, to serve on juries, and to adjudge your rights, then support Mr. Lincoln and the Black Republican party, who are in favor of the citizenship of the negro. ("Never, never.") For one, I am opposed to negro citizenship in any and every form. (Cheers.) I believe this government was made on the white basis. ("Good.") I believe it was made by white men, for the benefit of white men and their posterity for ever, and I am in favor of confining citizenship to white men, men of European birth and descent, instead of conferring it upon negroes, Indians and other inferior races. ("Good for you." "Douglas forever.")

Mr. Lincoln, following the example and lead of all the little Abolition orators, who go around and lecture in the basements of schools and churches, reads from the Declaration of Independence, that all men were created equal, and then asks how can you deprive a negro of that equality which God and the Declaration of Independence awards to him. He and they maintain that negro equality is guarantied by the laws of God, and that it is asserted in the Declaration of Independence. If they think so, of course they have a right to say so, and so vote. I do not question Mr. Lincoln's conscientious belief that the negro was made his equal, and hence is his brother, (laughter,) but for my own part, I do not regard the negro as my equal, and positively deny that he is my brother or any kin to me whatever. ("Never." "Hit him again," and cheers.) Lincoln has evidently learned by heart Parson Lovejoy's catechism. (Laughter and applause.) He can repeat it as well as Farnsworth, and he is worthy of a medal from father Giddings and Fred Douglass for his Abolitionism. (Laughter.) He holds that the negro was born his equal and yours, and that he was endowed with equality by the Almighty, and that no human law can deprive him of these rights which were guarantied to him by the Supreme ruler of the Universe. Now, I do not believe that the Almighty ever intended the negro to be the equal of the white man. ("Never, never.") If he did, he has been a long time demonstrating the fact. (Cheers.) For thousands of years the negro has been a race upon the earth, and during all that time, in all latitudes and climates, wherever he has wandered or been taken, he has been inferior to the race which he has there met. He belongs to an inferior race, and must always occupy an inferior position. ("Good," "that's so," &c.) I do not hold that because the negro is our inferior that therefore he ought to be a slave. By no means can such a conclusion be drawn from what I have said. On the contrary, I hold that humanity and christianity both require that the negro shall have and enjoy every right, every privilege, and every immunity consistent with the safety of the society in which he lives. (That's so.) On that point, I presume, there can be no diversity of opinion. You and I are bound to extend to our inferior and dependent being every right, every privilege, every facility and immunity consistent with the public good. The question then arises what rights and privileges are consistent with the public good. This is a question which each State and each Territory must decide for itself—Illinois has decided it for herself. We have provided that the negro shall not be a slave, and we have also provided that he shall not be a citizen, but protect him in his civil rights, in his life, his person and his property, only depriving him of all political rights whatsoever, and refusing to put him on an equality with the white man. ("Good.") That policy of Illinois is satisfactory to the Democratic party and to me . . .

Mr. Lincoln's reply:

.   .   .   .   .

Now gentlemen, I don't want to read at any greater length, but this is the true complexion of all I have ever said in regard to the institution of slavery and the black race. This is the whole of it, and anything that argues me into his idea of perfect social and political equality with the negro, is but a specious and fantastic arrangement of words, by which a man can prove a horse chestnut to be a chestnut horse. [Laughter.] I will say here, while upon this subject, that I have no purpose directly or indirectly to interfere with the institution of slavery in the States where it exists. I believe I have no lawful right to do so, and I have no inclination to do so. I have no purpose to introduce political and social equality between the white and the black races. There is a physical difference between the two, which in my judgment will probably forever forbid their living together upon the footing of perfect equality, and inasmuch as it becomes a necessity that there must be a difference, I, as well as Judge Douglas, am in favor of the race to which I belong, having the superior position. I have never said anything to the contrary, but I hold that notwithstanding all this, there is no reason in the world why the negro is not entitled to all the natural rights enumerated in the Declaration of Independence, the right to life, liberty and the pursuit of happiness. [Loud cheers.] I hold that he is as much entitled to these as the white man. I agree with Judge Douglas he is not my equal in many respects—certainly not in color, perhaps not in moral or intellectual endowment. But in the right to eat the bread, without leave of anybody else, which his own hand earns, *he is my equal and the equal of Judge Douglas, and the equal of every living man.* [Great applause.]

.   .   .   .   .

14

Second Debate with
Stephen A. Douglas at Freeport, Illinois[1]

August 27, 1858

Mr. Lincoln's Speech:

LADIES AND GENTLEMEN—On Saturday last, Judge Douglas and myself first met in public discussion. He spoke one hour, I an hour-and-a-half, and he replied for half an hour. The order is now reversed. I am to speak an hour, he an hour-and-a-half, and then I am to reply for half an hour. I propose to devote myself during the first hour to the scope of what was brought within the range of his half hour speech at Ottawa. Of course there was brought within the scope in that half hour's speech something of his own opening speech. In the course of that opening argument Judge Douglas proposed to me seven distinct interrogatories. In my speech of an hour and a half, I attended to some other parts of his speech, and incidentally, as I thought, answered one of the interrogatories then. I then distinctly intimated to him that I would answer the rest of his interrogatories on condition only that he should agree to answer as many for me. He made no intimation at the time of the proposition, nor did he in his reply allude at all to that suggestion of mine. I do him no injustice in saying that he occupied at least half of his reply in dealing with me as though I had *refused* to answer his interrogatories. I now propose that I will answer any of the interrogatories, upon condition that he will answer questions from me not exceeding the same number. I give him an opportunity to respond. The Judge remains silent. I now say to you that I will answer his interrogatories, whether he answers mine or not; [applause] and that after I have done so, I shall propound mine to him. [Applause.]

.   .   .   .   .

As to the first one, in regard to the Fugitive Slave Law, I have never hesitated to say, and I do not now hesitate to say, that I think,

---

[1] Debates Scrapbook, in *Collected Works,* III, pp. 39, 41–42.

under the Constitution of the United States, the people of the Southern States are entitled to a Congressional Fugitive Slave Law. Having said that, I have had nothing to say in regard to the existing Fugitive Slave Law further than that I think it should have been framed so as to be free from some of the objections that pertain to it, without lessening its efficiency. And inasmuch as we are not now in an agitation in regard to an alteration or modification of that law, I would not be the man to introduce it as a new subject of agitation upon the general question of slavery.

In regard to the other question of whether I am pledged to the admission of any more slave States into the Union, I state to you very frankly that I would be exceedingly sorry ever to be put in a position of having to pass upon that question. I should be exceedingly glad to know that there would never be another slave State admitted into the Union; [applause]; but I must add, that if slavery shall be kept out of the Territories during the territorial existence of any one given Territory, and then the people shall, having a fair chance and a clear field, when they come to adopt the Constitution, do such an extraordinary thing as to adopt a Slave Constitution, uninfluenced by the actual presence of the institution among them, I see no alternative, if we own the country, but to admit them into the Union. [Applause.]

. . . . .

. . . [I]n regard to the abolition of slavery in the District of Columbia. In relation to that, I have my mind very distinctly made up. I should be exceedingly glad to see slavery abolished in the District of Columbia. [Cries of "good, good."] I believe that Congress possesses the constitutional power to abolish it. Yet as a member of Congress, I should not with my present views, be in favor of *endeavoring* to abolish slavery in the District of Columbia, unless it would be upon these conditions. *First,* that the abolition should be gradual. *Second,* that it should be on a vote of the majority of qualified voters in the District, and *third,* that compensation should be made to unwilling owners. With these three conditions, I confess I would be exceedingly glad to see Congress abolish slavery in the District of Columbia, and, in the language of Henry Clay, "sweep from our Capital that foul blot upon our nation." [Loud applause.]

In regard to the fifth interrogatory, I must say here, that as to the question of the abolition of the Slave Trade between the different States, I can truly answer, as I have, that I am *pledged* to nothing about it. It is a subject to which I have not given that mature consideration that would make me feel authorized to state a position so as to hold myself entirely bound by it. In other words, that question has never been prominently enough before me to induce me to investigate whether we really have the Constitutional power to do it. I could investigate it if I had sufficient time, to bring myself to a conclusion upon that subject, but I have not done so, and I say so frankly to you here, and to Judge Douglas. I must say, however, that if I should be of opinion that Congress does possess the Constitutional power to abolish the slave trade among the different States, I should still not be in favor of the exercise of that power unless upon some conservative principle as I conceive it, akin to what I have said in relation to the abolition of slavery in the District of Columbia.

My answer as to whether I desire that slavery should be prohibited in all the Territories of the United States is full and explicit within itself, and cannot be made clearer by any comments of mine. So I suppose in regard to the question whether I am opposed to the acquisition of any more territory unless slavery is first prohibited therein, my answer is such that I could add nothing by way of illustration, or making myself better understood, than the answer which I have placed in writing.[2]

Now in all this, the Judge has me and he has me on the record. I suppose he had flattered himself that I was really entertaining one set of opinions for one place and another set for another place—that I was afraid to say at one place what I uttered at another. What I am saying here I suppose I say to a vast audience as strongly tending to Abolitionism as any audience in the State of Illinois, and I believe I am saying that which, if it would be offensive to any persons and render them enemies to myself, would be offensive to persons in this audience.

.   .   .   .   .

---

[2] Lincoln's written reply to this query was as follows: "I am impliedly, if not expressly, pledged to a belief in the *right* and *duty* of Congress to prohibit slavery in all the United States territories." (*Collected Works,* III, p. 40.)

15

Speech at Carlinville, Illinois[1]

August 31, 1858

He [Lincoln] said the question is often asked, why this fuss about niggers? It is dictated that their position is a small matter, but let us inquire whether it is or not. . . .

. . . . .

. . . There is no allusion to slavery in the constitution—and Madison says it was omitted that future generations might not know such a thing ever existed—and that the constitution might yet be a "national charter of freedom." And Keitt of S.C., once admitted that nobody ever thought it would exist to this day.

If placed in the former attitude we should have peace. But it is now advancing to become lawful everywhere. The Nebraska bill introduced this era—and it was gotten up by a man who twice voted for the Wilmot Proviso and the extension of the Missouri Compromise line to the Pacific. This change in our national policy is decided to be constitutional—although the court would not decide the only question before them—whether Dred Scott was a slave or not—and did decide, too, that a territorial legislature cannot exclude slavery in behalf of the people, and if their premises be correct a state cannot exclude it—for they tell us that the negro is property anywhere in the light that horses are property, and if the constitution gives the master a right of property in negroes above the jurisdiction of the territorial laws, enacted in the sovereignty of the people—it only requires another case and another favorable decision from the same court to make the rights of property alike in states as well as territories, and that by virtue of the

---

[1] Carlinville *Democrat,* September 2, 1858, in *Collected Works,* III, pp. 77–78.

constitution and in disregard of local laws to the contrary—Buchanan takes this position now. Sustain these men and negro equality will be abundant, as every white laborer will have occasion to regret when he is elbowed from his plow or his anvil by slave niggers.

.   .   .   .   .

16

Fourth Debate with Stephen A. Douglas at Charleston, Illinois[1]

September 18, 1858

Mr. Lincoln's Speech:

LADIES AND GENTLEMEN: It will be very difficult for an audience so large as this to hear distinctly what a speaker says, and consequently it is important that as profound silence be preserved as possible.

While I was at the hotel to-day an elderly gentleman called upon me to know whether I was really in favor of producing a perfect equality between the negroes and white people. [Great laughter.] While I had not proposed to myself on this occasion to say much on that subject, yet as the question was asked me I thought I would occupy perhaps five minutes in saying something in regard to it. I will say then that I am not, nor ever have been in favor of bringing about in any way the social and political equality of the white and black races, [applause]—that I am not nor ever have been in favor of making voters or jurors of negroes, nor of qualifying them to hold office, nor to intermarry with white people; and I will say in addition to this that

---

[1] Debates Scrapbook, in *Collected Works*, III, pp. 145–146, 178–181.

there is a physical difference between the white and black races which I believe will for ever forbid the two races living together on terms of social and political equality. And inasmuch as they cannot so live, while they do remain together there must be the position of superior and inferior, and I as much as any other man am in favor of having the superior position assigned to the white race. I say upon this occasion I do not perceive that because the white man is to have the superior position the negro should be denied everything. I do not understand that because I do not want a negro woman for a slave I must necessarily want her for a wife. [Cheers and laughter.] My understanding is that I can just let her alone. I am now in my fiftieth year, and I certainly never have had a black woman for either a slave or a wife. So it seems to me quite possible for us to get along without making either slaves or wives of negroes. I will add to this that I have never seen to my knowledge a man, woman or child who was in favor of producing a perfect equality, social and political, between negroes and white men. I recollect of but one distinguished instance that I ever heard of so frequently as to be entirely satisfied of its correctness— and that is the case of Judge Douglas' old friend Col. Richard M. Johnson.[2] [Laughter.] I will also add to the remarks I have made, (for I am not going to enter at large upon this subject,) that I have never had the least apprehension that I or my friends would marry negroes if there was no law to keep them from it, [laughter] but as Judge Douglas and his friends seem to be in great apprehension that they might, if there were no law to keep them from it, [roars of laughter] I give him the most solemn pledge that I will to the very last stand by the law of this State, which forbids the marrying of white people with negroes. [Continued laughter and applause.] I will add one further word, which is this, that I do not understand there is any place where an alteration of the social and political relations of the negro and the white man can be made except in the State Legislature—not in the Congress of the United States—and as I do not really apprehend the approach of any such thing myself, and as Judge Douglas seems to be in constant horror that some such danger is rapidly approaching, I propose as the best means to prevent it that the Judge be kept at home and placed in the State Legislature to fight the measure.

---

[2] Former Vice-President Richard Johnson and a black woman lived together as man and wife for many years at a time when interracial marriages were prohibited.

[Uproarious laughter and applause.] I do not propose dwelling longer at this time on this subject.

.   .   .   .   .

[After Lincoln spoke for an hour, Douglas spoke for an hour and a half. Lincoln was then given a chance to reply.]

Mr. Lincoln's Rejoinder:

Fellow Citizens—It follows as a matter of course that a half-hour answer to a speech of an hour-and-a-half can be but a very hurried one. I shall only be able to touch upon a few of the points suggested by Judge Douglas, and give them a brief attention, while I shall have to totally omit others for the want of time.

Judge Douglas has said to you that he has not been able to get from me an answer to the question whether I am in favor of negro-citizenship. So far as I know, the Judge never asked me the question before. [Applause.] He shall have no occasion to ever ask it again, for I tell him very frankly that I am not in favor of negro citizenship. [Renewed applause.] This furnishes me an occasion for saying a few words upon the subject. I mentioned in a certain speech of mine which has been printed, that the Supreme Court had decided that a negro could not possibly be made a citizen, and without saying what was my ground of complaint in regard to that, or whether I had any ground of complaint, Judge Douglas has from that thing manufactured nearly every thing that he ever says about my disposition to produce an equality between the negroes and the white people. [Laughter and applause.] If any one will read my speech, he will find I mentioned that as one of the points decided in the course of the Supreme Court opinions, but I did not state what objection I had to it. But Judge Douglas tells the people what my objection was when I did not tell them myself. [Loud applause and laughter.] Now my opinion is that the different States have the power to make a negro a citizen under the Constitution of the United States if they choose. The Dred Scott decision decides that they have not that power. If the State of Illinois had that power I should be opposed to the exercise of it. [Cries of "good," "good," and applause.] That is all I have to say about it.

Judge Douglas has told me that he heard my speeches north and my speeches south—that he had heard me at Ottawa and at Freeport in the north, and recently at Jonesboro in the south, and there was a very different cast of sentiment in the speeches made at the different points. I will not charge upon Judge Douglas that he wilfully misrepresents me, but I call upon every fair-minded man to take these speeches and read them, *and I dare him to point out any difference between my printed speeches north and south.* [Great cheering.] While I am here perhaps I ought to say a word, if I have the time, in regard to the latter portion of the Judge's speech, which was a sort of declamation in reference to my having said I entertained the belief that this government would not endure, half slave and half free. I have said so and I did not say it without what seemed to me to be good reasons. It perhaps would require more time than I have now to set forth these reasons in detail; but let me ask you a few questions. Have we ever had any peace on this slavery question? [No, no.] When are we to have peace upon it if it is kept in the position it now occupies? [Never.] . . . [T]here is no way of putting an end to the slavery agitation amongst us but to put it back upon the basis where our fathers placed it, [applause] no way but to keep it out of our new Territories [renewed applause]—to restrict it forever to the old States where it now exists. [Tremendous and prolonged cheering; cries of "That's the doctrine," "Good," "Good," &c.] Then the public mind *will* rest in the belief that it is in the course of ultimate extinction. That is one way of putting an end to the slavery agitation. [Applause.]

The other way is for us to surrender and let Judge Douglas and his friends have their way and plant slavery over all the States— cease speaking of it as in any way a wrong—regard slavery as one of the common matters of property, and speak of negroes as we do of our horses and cattle. But while it drives on in its state of progress as it is now driving, and as it has driven for the last five years, I have ventured the opinion, and I say to-day, that we will have no end to the slavery agitation until it takes one turn or the other. [Applause.] I do not mean that when it takes a turn towards ultimate extinction it will be in a day, nor in a year, nor in two years. I do not suppose that in the most peaceful way ultimate extinction would occur in less than a hundred years at the least; but that it will occur in the best way for both races in God's own good time, I have no doubt. [Applause.] But, my friends, I have used up more of my time than I intended on this point.

.   .   .   .   .

17

Fifth Debate with
Stephen A. Douglas at Galesburg, Illinois[1]

October 7, 1858

Mr. Douglas' Speech:

. . . . .

. . . My friend Lincoln finds its extremely difficult to manage a debate in the centre part of the State, where there is a mixture of men from the North and the South. In the extreme northern part of Illinois he can proclaim as bold and radical abolitionism as ever Giddings, Lovejoy, or Garrison enunciated, but when he gets down a little further South he claims that he is an old line Whig, (great laughter,) a disciple of Henry Clay, ("Singleton says he defeated Clay's nomination for the Presidency," and cries of "that's so,") and declares that he still adheres to the old line Whig creed, and has nothing whatever to do with Abolitionism, or negro equality, or negro citizenship. ("Hurrah for Douglas.") I once before hinted this of Mr. Lincoln in a public speech, and at Charleston he defied me to show that there was any difference between his speeches in the North and in the South, and that they were not in strict harmony. I will now call your attention to two of them, and you can then say whether you would be apt to believe that the same man ever uttered both. (Laughter and cheers.) In a speech in reply to me at Chicago in July last, Mr. Lincoln, in speaking of the equality of the negro with the white man used the following language:

> I should like to know, if taking this old Declaration of Independence, which declares that all men are equal upon principle, and making exceptions to it, where will it stop? If one man says it does not

---

[1] Debates Scrapbook, in *Collected Works*, III, pp. 213–215, 221–222.

mean a negro, why may not another man say it does not mean another man? (Laughter.) If the Declaration is not the truth, let us get the statute book in which we find it and tear it out. Who is so bold as to do it? If it is not true, let us tear it out.

You find that Mr. Lincoln there proposed that if the doctrine of the Declaration of Independence, declaring all men to be born equal, did not include the negro and put him on an equality with the white man, that we should take the statute book and tear it out. (Laughter and cheers.) He there took the ground that the negro race is included in the Declaration of Independence as the equal of the white race, and that there could be no such thing as a distinction in the races, making one superior and the other inferior. I read now from the same speech:

> My friends, [he says,] I have detained you about as long as I desire to do, and I have only to say let us discard all this quibbling about this man and the other man—this race and that race, and the other race being inferior and therefore they must be placed in an inferior position, discarding our standard that we have left us. Let us discard all these things, and unite as one people throughout this land, until we shall once more stand up declaring that all men are created equal.

("That's right," &c.)

Yes, I have no doubt that you think it is right, but the Lincoln men down in Coles, Tazewell and Sangamon counties *do not* think it is right. (Immense applause and laughter. Hit him again, &c.) In the conclusion of the same speech, talking to the Chicago Abolitionists, he said: "I leave you, hoping that the lamp of liberty will burn in your bosoms until there shall no longer be a doubt that all men are created free and equal." (Good, good, shame, &c.) Well, you say good to that, and you are going to vote for Lincoln because he holds that doctrine. ("That's so.") I will not blame you for supporting him on that ground, but I will show you in immediate contrast with that doctrine, what Mr. Lincoln said down in Egypt in order to get votes in that locality where they do not hold to such a doctrine. In a joint discussion between Mr. Lincoln and myself, at Charleston, I think, on the 18th of last month, Mr. Lincoln referring to this subject used the following language:

> I will say then, that I am not nor never have been in favor of bringing about in any way, the social and political equality of the white and black races; that I am not nor never have been in favor of making

voters of the free negroes, or jurors, or qualifying them to hold office, or having them to marry with white people. I will say in addition, that there is a physical difference between the white and black races, which, I suppose, will forever forbid the two races living together upon terms of social and political equality, and inasmuch as they cannot so live, that while they do remain together, there must be the position of superior and inferior, that I as much as any other white man am in favor of the superior position being assigned to the white man.

(Good for Lincoln.)

Fellow-citizens, here you find men hurrahing for Lincoln and saying that he did right, when in one part of the State he stood up for negro equality, and in another part for political effect, discarded the doctrine and declared that there always must be a superior and inferior race. (They're not men. Put them out, &c.) Abolitionists up north are expected and required to vote for Lincoln because he goes for the equality of the races, holding that by the Declaration of Independence the white man and the negro were created equal and endowed by the Divine law with that equality, and down south he tells the old Whigs, the Kentuckians, Virginians, and Tennesseeans, that there is a physical difference in the races, making one superior and the other inferior, and that he is in favor of maintaining the superiority of the white race over the negro. Now, how can you reconcile those two positions of Mr. Lincoln? He is to be voted for in the South as a pro-slavery man, and he is to be voted for in the North as an Abolitionist. . . .

.   .   .   .   .

Mr. Lincoln's Reply

.   .   .   .   .

Now a few words in regard to these extracts from speeches of mine, which Judge Douglas has read to you, and which he supposes are in very great contrast to each other. Those speeches have been before the public for a considerable time, and if they have any inconsistency in them, if there is any conflict in them the public have been able to detect it. When the Judge says, in speaking on this subject, that I make speeches of one sort for the people of the Northern end of the State, and of a different sort for the Southern people, he assumes that I do not understand that my speeches will be put in print and read North and South. I knew all the while that the speech that I made at Chicago and the one I made at Jonesboro and the one at Charleston, would all be put in print and all the reading and intelligent men in the community would see them and know all about my opinions. And I have not supposed, and do not now suppose, that there is any conflict whatever between them. ["They are all good speeches!" "Hurrah for Lincoln!"] But the Judge will have it that if we do not confess that there is a sort of inequality between the white and black races, which justifies us in making them slaves, we must, then, insist that there is a degree of equality that requires us to make them our wives. [Loud applause, and cries, "Give it to him;" "Hit him again."] Now, I have all the while taken a broad distinction in regard to that matter; and that is all there is in these different speeches which he arrays here, and the entire reading of either of the speeches will show that that distinction was made. Perhaps by taking two parts of the same speech, he could have got up as much of a conflict as the one he has found. I have all the while maintained, that in so far as it should be insisted that there was an equality between the white and black races that should produce a perfect social and political equality, it was an impossibility. This you have seen in my printed speeches, and with it I have said, that in their right to "life, liberty and the pursuit of happiness," as proclaimed in that old Declaration, the inferior races are our equals. [Long-continued cheering.] And these declarations I have constantly made in reference to the abstract moral question, to contemplate and consider when we are legislating about any new country which is not already cursed with the actual presence of the evil—slavery. I have never manifested any impatience with the necessities that spring from the actual presence of black people amongst us, and the actual existence of slavery amongst us where it does already exist; but I have insisted that, in legislating for new countries, where it does not exist, there is no just rule other than that of moral and abstract right! With reference to those new countries, those maxims as to the right of a people to "life, liberty and the pursuit of happiness," were the just rules to be constantly referred to. There is no misunderstanding this, except by men interested to misunderstand it. [Applause.] I take it that I have to address an intelligent and reading community, who will peruse what I say, weigh it, and then judge whether I advance improper or unsound views, or whether I advance hypocritical, and deceptive, and contrary views in different portions of the country. I believe myself to be guilty of no such thing as the latter, though, of course, I cannot claim that I am entirely free from all error in the opinions I advance.

.   .   .   .   .

18

Seventh and Last Debate with Stephen A. Douglas at Alton, Illinois[1]

October 15, 1858

.   .   .   .   .

Mr. Lincoln's Reply

.   .   .   .   .

But is it true that all the difficulty and agitation we have in regard to this institution of slavery springs from office seeking—from the mere ambition of politicians? Is that the truth? How many times have we had danger from this question? Go back to the day of the Missouri Compromise. Go back to the Nullification question, at the bottom of which lay this same slavery question. Go back to the time of the Annexation of Texas. Go back to the troubles that led to the Compromise of 1850. You will find that every time, with the single exception of the Nullification question, they sprung from an endeavor to spread this institution. There never was a party in the history of this country, and there probably never will be of sufficient strength to disturb the general peace of the country. Parties themselves may be divided and quarrel on minor questions, yet it extends not beyond the

---

[1] Debates Scrapbook, in *Collected Works,* III, pp. 310–313, 315–316.

---

parties themselves. But does *not* this question make a disturbance outside of political circles? Does it not enter into the churches and rend them asunder? What divided the great Methodist Church into two parts, North and South? What has raised this constant disturbance in every Presbyterian General Assembly that meets? What disturbed the Unitarian Church in this very city two years ago? What has jarred and shaken the great American Tract Society recently, not yet splitting it, but sure to divide it in the end. Is it not this same mighty, deep seated power that somehow operates on the minds of men, exciting and stirring them up in every avenue of society—in politics, in religion, in literature, in morals, in all the manifold relations of life? [Applause.] Is this the work of politicians? Is that irresistible power which for fifty years has shaken the government and agitated the people to be stilled and subdued by pretending that it is an exceedingly simple thing, and we ought not to talk about it? [Great cheers and laughter.] If you will get everybody else to stop talking about it, I assure I will quit before they have half done so. [Renewed laughter.] But where is the philosophy or statesmanship which assumes that you can quiet that disturbing element in our society which has disturbed us for more than half a century, which has been the only serious danger that has threatened our institutions—I say, where is the philosophy or the statesmanship based on the assumption that we are to quit talking about it [applause], and that the public mind is all at once to cease being agitated by it? Yet this is the policy here in the North that Douglas is advocating—that we are to care nothing about it! I ask you if it is not a false philosophy? Is it not a false statesmanship that undertakes to build up a system of policy upon the basis of caring nothing about *the very thing that every body does care the most about?* ["Yes, yes," and applause]—a thing which all experience has shown we care a very great deal about? [Laughter and applause.]

.   .   .   .   .

Now irrespective of the moral aspect of this question as to whether there is a right or wrong in enslaving a negro, I am still in favor of our new Territories being in such a condition that white men may find a home—may find some spot where they can better their condition—where they can settle upon new soil and better their condition in life. [Great and continued cheering.] I am in favor of this not merely, (I must say it here as I have elsewhere,) for our own people who are born amongst us, but as an outlet for *free white people everywhere,* the world over—in which Hans and Baptiste and Patrick, and all other men from all the world, may find new homes and better their conditions in life. [Loud and long continued applause.]

I have stated upon former occasions, and I may as well state again, what I understand to be the real issue in this controversy between Judge Douglas and myself. On the point of my wanting to make war between the free and the slave States, there has been no issue between us. So, too, when he assumes that I am in favor of introducing a perfect social and political equality between the white and black races. These are false issues, upon which Judge Douglas has tried to force the controversy. There is no foundation in truth for the charge that I maintain either of these propositions. The real issue in this controversy—the one pressing upon every mind—is the sentiment on the part of one class that looks upon the institution of slavery *as a wrong,* and of another class that *does not* look upon it as a wrong. The sentiment that contemplates the institution of slavery in this country as a wrong is the sentiment of the Republican party. It is the sentiment around which all their actions—all their arguments circle—from which all their propositions radiate. They look upon it as being a moral, social and political wrong; and while they contemplate it as such, they nevertheless have due regard for its actual existence among us, and the difficulties of getting rid of it in any satisfactory way and to all the constitutional obligations thrown about it. Yet having a due regard for these, they desire a policy in regard to it that looks to its not creating any more danger. They insist that it should as far as may be, *be treated* as a wrong, and one of the methods of treating it as a wrong is to *make provision that it shall grow no larger.* [Loud applause.] They also desire a policy that looks to a peaceful end of slavery at sometime, as being wrong. These are the views they entertain in regard to it as I understand them; and all their sentiments—all their arguments and propositions are brought within this range. I have said and I repeat it here, that if there be a man amongst us who does not think that the institution of slavery is wrong in any one of the aspects of which I have spoken, he is misplaced and ought not to be with us. And if there be a man amongst us who is so impatient of it as a wrong as to disregard its actual presence among us and the difficulty of getting rid of it suddenly in a satisfactory way, and to disregard the constitutional obligations thrown about it, that man is misplaced if he is on our platform. We disclaim sympathy with him in practical action. He is not placed properly with us.

On this subject of treating it as a wrong, and limiting its spread, let me say a word. Has any thing ever threatened the existence of this Union save and except this very institution of Slavery? What is it that we hold most dear amongst us? Our own liberty and prosperity. What has ever threatened our liberty and prosperity save and except this institution of Slavery? If this is true, how do you propose to improve the condition of things by enlarging Slavery—by spreading it out and making it bigger? You may have a wen or a cancer upon your person and not be able to cut it out lest you bleed to death; but surely it is no way to cure it, to engraft it and spread it over your whole body. That is no proper way of treating what you regard a wrong. You see this peaceful way of dealing with it as a wrong—restricting the spread of it, and not allowing it to go into new countries where it has not already existed. That is the peaceful way, the old-fashioned way, the way in which the fathers themselves set us the example.

On the other hand, I have said there is a sentiment which treats it as *not* being wrong. That is the Democratic sentiment of this day. . . .

. . . . .

That is the real issue. That is the issue that will continue in this country when these poor tongues of Judge Douglas and myself shall be silent. It is the eternal struggle between these two principles—right and wrong—throughout the world. They are the two principles that have stood face to face from the beginning of time; and will ever continue to struggle. The one is the common right of humanity and the other the divine right of kings. It is the same principle in whatever shape it develops itself. It is the same spirit that says, "You work and toil and earn bread, and I'll eat it." [Loud applause.] No matter in what shape it comes, whether from the mouth of a king who seeks to bestride the people of his own nation and live by the fruit of their labor, or from one race of men as an apology for enslaving another race, it is the same tyrannical principle. I was glad to express my gratitude at Quincy, and I reexpress it here to Judge Douglas—*that he looks to no end of the institution of slavery*. That will help the people to see where the struggle really is. It will hereafter place with us all men who really do wish the wrong may have an end. And whenever we can get rid of the fog which obscures the real question—when we can get Judge Douglas and his friends to avow a policy looking to its perpetuation—we can get out from among them that class of men and bring them to the side of those who treat it as a wrong. Then there will soon be an end of it, and that end will be its "ultimate extinction." Whenever the issue can be distinctly made, and all extraneous matter thrown out so that men can fairly see the real difference between the parties, this controversy will soon be settled, and it will be done peaceably too. There will be no war, no violence. It will be placed again where the wisest and best men of the world, placed it. Brooks of South Carolina once declared that when this Constitution was framed, its framers did not look to the institution existing until this day. When he said this, I think he stated a fact that is fully borne out by the history of the times. But he also said they were better and wiser men than the men of these days; yet the men of these days had experience which they had not, and by the invention of the cotton gin it became a necessity in this country that slavery should be perpetual. I now say that willingly or unwillingly, purposely or without purpose, Judge Douglas has been the most prominent instrument in changing the position of the institution of slavery which the fathers of the government expected to come to an end ere this—*and putting it upon Brooks' cotton gin basis,* [Great applause,]—placing it where he openly confesses he has no desire there shall ever be an end of it. [Renewed applause.]

.   .   .   .   .

19

To Elihu B. Washburne[1]

Springfield
January 29, 1859

Hon. E. B. Washburne.
My dear Sir

I have just received your brother's speech sent me by yourself. I had read it before; and you will oblige me by presenting him with

[1] Signed autograph letter, owned by Douglas S. Brown, Elm Grove, Wisconsin, in *Collected Works,* III, p. 351. Elihu Washburne was a Republican Congressman from Illinois; the speech that Lincoln refers to was delivered by Representative Israel Washburn, Jr. of Maine, on January 10, 1859.

my respects, and telling him I doubly thank him for making it—first, because the points are so just and well put; and next, because it is so well timed. We needed, from some one who can get the public attention, just such a speech just at this time. His objection to the Oregon constitution because it excludes free negroes, is the only thing I wish he had omitted. Your friend as ever

A. LINCOLN

20

To Salmon P. Chase[1]

Springfield, Illinois
June 9, 1859

Hon: S. P. Chase:
Dear Sir
Please pardon the liberty I take in addressing you, as I now do. It appears by the papers that the late Republican State convention of Ohio adopted a Platform, of which the following is one plank, "A repeal of the atrocious Fugitive Slave Law."

This is already damaging us here. I have no doubt that if that plank be even *introduced* into the next Republican National convention, it will explode it. Once introduced, its supporters and it's opponents will quarrel irreconcilably. The latter believe the U.S. constitution declares that a fugitive slave *"shall be delivered up";* and they look upon the above plank as dictated by the spirit which declares a fugitive slave *"shall not be delivered up"*

---

[1] Signed autograph letter, Historical Society of Pennsylvania, Philadelphia, Pennsylvania, in *Collected Works,* III, p. 384. Salmon P. Chase was one of the leaders of the Republican Party and was Governor of Ohio.

I enter upon no argument one way or the other; but I assure you the cause of Republicanism is hopeless in Illinois, if it be in any way made responsible for that plank. I hope you can, and will, contribute something to relieve us from it. Your Obt. Servt.

A. LINCOLN

21

Speech at Cincinnati, Ohio[1]

September 17, 1859

. . . . .

At . . . Memphis, he [Douglas] declared that while in all contests between the negro and the white man, he was for the white man, but that in all questions between the negro and the crocodile he was for the negro. (Laughter.) He did not make that declaration accidentally at Memphis. He made it a great many times in the canvass in Illinois last year, (though I don't know that it was reported in any of his speeches there,) but he frequently made it. I believe he repeated it at Columbus, and I should not wonder if he repeated it here. It is, then, a deliberate way of expressing himself upon that subject. It is a matter of mature deliberation with him thus to express himself upon that point of his case. It therefore requires some deliberate attention.

The first inference seems to be that if you do not enslave the negro you are wronging the white man in some way or other, and that whoever is opposed to the negro being enslaved is in some way or other against the white man. Is not that a falsehood? If there was a

[1] *Illinois State Journal,* October 7, 1859, in *Collected Works,* III, p. 445–446.

necessary conflict between the white man and the negro, I should be for the white man as much as Judge Douglas; but I say there is no such necessary conflict. I say that there is room enough for us all to be free, (loud manifestations of applause,) and that it not only does not wrong the white man that the negro should be free, but it positively wrongs the mass of the white men that the negro should be enslaved; that the mass of white men are really injured by the effect of slave labor in the vicinity of the fields of their own labor. (Applause.)

But I do not desire to dwell upon this branch of the question more than to say that this assumption of his is false, and I do hope that that fallacy will not long prevail in the minds of intelligent white men. At all events, you Kentuckians ought to thank Judge Douglas for it. It is for your benefit it is made.

The other branch of it is, that in a struggle between the negro and the crocodile, he is for the negro. Well, I don't know that there is any struggle between the negro and the crocodile, either. (Laughter.) I suppose that if a crocodile (or as we old Ohio river boatmen used to call them, alligators) should come across a white man, he would kill him if he could, and so he would a negro. But what, at last, is this proposition? I believe it is a sort of proposition in proportion, which may be stated thus: As the negro is to the white man, so is the crocodile to the negro, and as the negro may rightfully treat the crocodile as a beast or reptile, so the white man may rightfully treat the negro as a beast or a reptile. (Applause.) That is really the "knip" of all that argument of his.

Now, my brother Kentuckians, who believe in this, you ought to thank Judge Douglas for having put that in a much more taking way than any of yourselves have done. (Applause.)

.   .   .   .   .

22

Speech at New Haven, Connecticut[1]

March 6, 1860

．　　．　　．　　．　　．

. . . I am glad to see that a system of labor prevails in New England under which laborers CAN *strike* when they want to [Cheers,] where they are not obliged to work under all circumstances, and are not tied down and obliged to labor whether you pay them or not! [Cheers.] I *like* the system which lets a man quit when he wants to, and wish it might prevail everywhere. [Tremendous applause.] One of the reasons why I am opposed to Slavery is just here. What is the true condition of the laborer? I take it that it is best for all to leave each man free to acquire property as fast as he can. Some will get wealthy. I don't believe in a law to prevent a man from getting rich; it would do more harm than good. So while we do not propose any war upon capital, we do wish to allow the humblest man an equal chance to get rich with everybody else. [Applause.] When one starts poor, as most do in the race of life, free society is such that he knows he can better his condition; he knows that there is no fixed condition of labor, for his whole life. I am not ashamed to confess that twenty five years ago I was a hired laborer, mauling rails, at work on a flatboat—just what might happen to any poor man's son! [Applause.] I want every man to have the chance—and I believe a black man is entitled to it—in which he *can* better his condition—when he may look forward and hope to be a hired laborer this year and the next, work for himself afterward, and finally to hire men to work for him! That is the true system. Up here in New England, you have a soil that scarcely sprouts black-eyed beans, and yet where will you find wealthy men so wealthy, and poverty so rarely in extremity? There is not an-

---

[1] New Haven *Daily Palladium,* March 7, 1860, in *Collected Works,* IV, pp. 24–25.

---

other such place on earth! [Cheers.] I desire that if you get too thick here, and find it hard to better your condition on this soil, you may have a chance to strike and go somewhere else, where you may not be degraded, nor have your family corrupted by forced rivalry with negro slaves. I want you to have a clean bed, and no snakes in it! [Cheers.] Then you can better your condition, and so it may go on and on in one ceaseless round so long as man exists on the face of the earth! [Prolonged applause.]

.   .   .   .   .

23

Speech of H. Ford Douglass[1]

July 4, 1860

.   .   .   .   .

. . . We have four parties in this country that have marshalled themselves on the highway of American politics, asking for the votes of the American people to place them in possession of the government. We have what is called the Union party, led by Mr. Bell, of Tennessee; we have what is called the Democratic party, led by Stephen A. Douglas, of Illinois; we have the party called the Seceders, or the Slave-Code Democrats, led by John C. Breckinridge, of Kentucky, and then we have the Republican party, led by Abraham Lincoln, of Illinois. All of these parties ask for your support, because they profess to represent some principle. So far as the principles of freedom and the hopes of the black man are concerned, all these par-

---

[1] Douglass, a black abolitionist from Illinois, spoke at a mass meeting called by the Massachusetts Anti-Slavery Society. *The Liberator,* July 13, 1860.

---

ties are barren and unfruitful; neither of them seeks to lift the negro out of his fetters, and rescue this day from odium and disgrace.

Take Abraham Lincoln. I want to know if any man can tell me the difference between the anti-slavery of Abraham Lincoln, and the anti-slavery of the old Whig party, or the anti-slavery of Henry Clay? Why, there is no difference between them. Abraham Lincoln is simply a Henry Clay Whig, and he believes just as Henry Clay believed in regard to this question. And Henry Clay was just as odious to the anti-slavery cause and anti-slavery men as ever was John C. Calhoun. In fact, he did as much to perpetuate negro slavery in this country as any other man who has ever lived. Henry Clay once said, "That is property which the law declares to be property," and that "two hundred years of legislation have sanctioned and sanctified property in slaves"! Wherever Henry Clay is to-day in the universe of God, that atheistic lie is with him, with all its tormenting memories. (Applause.)

I know Abraham Lincoln, and I know something about his anti-slavery. I know the Republicans do not like this kind of talk, because, while they are willing to steal our thunder, they are unwilling to submit to the conditions imposed upon that party that assumes to be anti-slavery. They say that they cannot go as fast as you anti-slavery men go in this matter; that they cannot afford to be uncompromisingly honest, nor so radical as you Garrisonians; that they want to take time; that they want to do the work gradually. They say, "We must not be in too great a hurry to overthrow slavery; at least, we must take half a loaf, if we cannot get the whole." Now, my friends, I believe that the very best way to overthrow slavery in this country is to occupy the highest possible anti-slavery ground. Washington Irving tells a story of a Dutchman, who wanted to jump over a ditch, and he went back three miles in order to get a good start, and when he got up to the ditch, he had to sit down on the wrong side to get his breath. So it is with these political parties; they are compelled, they say, when they get up to the ditch of slavery, to stop and take breath.

I do not believe in the anti-slavery of Abraham Lincoln, because he is on the side of this Slave Power of which I am speaking, that has possession of the Federal Government. What does he propose to do? Simply to let the people and the Territories regulate their domestic institutions in their own way. In the great debate between Lincoln and Douglas in Illinois, when he was interrogated as to whether he was in favor of the admission of more slave States into the Union, he said, that so long as we owned the territories, he did not see any other way of doing than to admit those States when they made application,

WITH OR WITHOUT SLAVERY. Now, that is Douglas's doctrine; it is stealing the thunder of Stephen A. Douglas.

In regard to the repeal of the Fugitive Slave Law, Abraham Lincoln occupied the same position that the old Whig party occupied in 1852. They asserted then, in their platform, that they were not in favor of the repeal of that law, and that they would do nothing to lessen its efficiency. What did he say at Freeport? Why, that the South was entitled to a Fugitive Slave Law; and although he thought the law could be modified a little, yet, he said, if he was in Congress, he would have it done in such a way as *not to lessen its efficiency!* Here, then, is Abraham Lincoln in favor of carrying out that infamous Fugitive Slave Law, that not only strikes down the liberty of every black man in the United States, but virtually the liberty of every white man as well; for, under that law, there is not a man in this presence who might not be arrested to-day upon the simple testimony of one man, and, after an *ex parte* trial, hurried off to slavery and to chains. *Habeas corpus,* trial by jury,—those great bulwarks of freedom, reared by the blood and unspeakable woe of your English ancestors, amidst the conflicts of a thousand years,—are struck down by this law; and the man whose name is inscribed upon the Presidential banner of the Republican party is in favor of keeping it upon the statute-book!

Not only would I arraign Mr. Lincoln, in regard to that law, for his pro-slavery character and principles, but when he was a member of the House of Representatives, in 1849, on the 10th day of January, he went through the District of Columbia, and consulted the prominent pro-slavery men and slaveholders of the District, and then went into the House of Representatives, and introduced, on his own responsibility, a fugitive slave law for the District of Columbia. It is well known that the law of 1793 did not apply to the District, and it was necessary, in order that slaveholders might catch their slaves who sought safety under the shadow of the capitol, that a special law should be passed for the District of Columbia; and so Mr. Lincoln went down deeper into the pro-slavery pool than even Mr. Mason of Virginia did in the Fugitive Slave Law of 1850. Here, then, is the man who asks for your votes, and for the votes of the anti-slavery people of New England, who, on his own responsibility, without any temptation whatever, introduced into the District of Columbia a fugitive slave law! That is a fact for the consideration of anti-slavery men.

Then, there is another item which I want to bring out in this connection. I am a colored man; I am an American citizen; and I think that I am entitled to exercise the elective franchise. I am about twenty-eight years old, and I would like to vote very much. I think I am old enough to vote, and I think that, if I had a vote to give, I should know enough to place it on the side of freedom. (Applause.) No party, it seems to me, is entitled to the sympathy of anti-slavery men, unless that party is willing to extend to the black man all the rights of a citizen. I care nothing about that anti-slavery which wants to make the Territories free, while it is unwilling to extend to me, as a man, in the free States, all the rights of a man. (Applause.) In the State of Illinois, where I live—my adopted State—I have been laboring to make it a place fit for a decent man to live in. In that State, we have a code of black laws that would disgrace any Barbary State, or any uncivilized people in the far-off islands of the sea. Men of my complexion are not allowed to testify in a court of justice, where a white man is a party. If a white man happens to owe me anything, unless I can prove it by the testimony of a white man, I cannot collect the debt. Now, two years ago, I went through the State of Illinois for the purpose of getting signers to a petition, asking the Legislature to repeal the "Testimony Law," so as to permit colored men to testify against white men. I went to prominent Republicans, and among others, to Abraham Lincoln and Lyman Trumbull, and neither of them dared to sign that petition, to give me the right to testify in a court of justice! ("Hear, hear.") In the State of Illinois, they tax the colored people for every conceivable purpose. They tax the negro's property to support schools for the education of the white man's children, but the colored people are not permitted to enjoy any of the benefits resulting from that taxation. We are compelled to impose upon ourselves additional taxes, in order to educate our children. The State lays its iron hand upon the negro, holds him down, and puts the other hand into his pocket and steals his hard earnings, to educate the children of white men; and if we sent our children to school, Abraham Lincoln would kick them out, in the name of Republicanism and anti-slavery!

.   .   .   .   .

THREE

The Presidency: Colonization and Emancipation (1860–1863)

Even before his inauguration as President, Lincoln was called upon to make some fundamental decisions. As the southern states began their trek out of the union, Lincoln was under great pressure to offer some compromise proposals yet, at the same time, he was in danger of losing the support of anti-slavery men in his own party if he surrendered on the issue of slavery expansion. After he became President, Lincoln had to deal with crucial issues concerning slavery while he was in the midst of war, knowing that the loyalty of the slave-owning border states was tenuous, but crucial. As President of a tragically divided nation, Lincoln was always conscious of the fact that his decisions on slavery might further divide public opinion and dilute the strength of the Union. In this context, Lincoln faced a series of questions: should fugitive slaves of Confederate masters be returned? Should the North offer southern slaves their freedom in order to secure their help in the war effort? If emancipation became a Union policy should loyal slaveowners be offered compensation for their property losses? And, finally, what should be done with newly freed Negroes; should they be colonized outside of the United States?

24

Frederick Douglass: "The Late Election" [1]

December 1860

. . . The clamor now raised by the slaveholders about "Northern aggression," "sectional warfare," as a pretext of dissolving the Union, has this basis only: The Northern people have elected, against the opposition of the slaveholding South, a man for President who declared his opposition to the further extension of slavery over the soil belonging to the United States. Such is the head and front, and the full extent of the offense, for which "minute men" are forming, drums are beating, flags are flying, people are arming, "banks are closing," "stocks are falling," and the South generally taking on dreadfully.

By referring to another part of our present monthly, our respected readers will find a few samples of the spirit of the Southern press on the subject. They are full of intrigue, smell of brimstone, and betoken a terrific explosion. Unquestionably, "secession," "disunion," "Southern Confederacy," and the like phrases, are the most popular political watch words of the cotton-growing States of the Union. Nor is this sentiment to be entirely despised. If Mr. Lincoln were really an Abolition President, which he is not; if he were a friend to the Abolition movement, instead of being, as he is, its most powerful enemy, the dissolution of the Union might be the only effective mode of perpetuating slavery in the Southern States—since if it could succeed, it would place slavery beyond the power of the President and his Government. But the South has now no such cause for disunion. The present alarm and perturbation will cease; the Southern fire-eaters will be appeased and will retrace their steps.—There is no sufficient cause for the dissolution of the Union. Whoever lives through the next four years will see Mr. Lincoln and his Administration attacked more bitterly for their pro-slavery truckling, than for doing any anti-slavery work. He

---

[1] *Douglass' Monthly,* December 1860, pp. 370–371. Frederick Douglass, an ex-slave, was the most famous of the black abolitionists.

---

and his party will become the best protectors of slavery where it now is, and just such protectors as slaveholders will most need. In order to defeat him, the slaveholders took advantage of the ignorance and stupidity of the masses, and assured them that Lincoln is an Abolitionist. This, Mr. Lincoln and his party will lose no time in scattering to the winds as false and groundless. With the single exception of the question of slavery extension, Mr. Lincoln proposes no measure which can bring him into antagonistic collision with the traffickers in human flesh, either in the States or in the District of Columbia. The Union will, therefore, be saved simply because there is no cause in the election of Mr. Lincoln for its dissolution. Slavery will be as safe, and safer, in the Union under such a President, than it can be under any President of a Southern Confederacy. This is our impression, and we deeply regret the facts from which it is derived.

With an Abolition President we should consider a successful separation of the slave from the free States a calamity, greatly damaging to the prospects of our long enslaved, bruised and mutilated people; but under what may be expected of the Republican party, with its pledges to put down the slaves should they attempt to rise, and to hunt them should they run away, a dissolution of the Union would be highly beneficial to the cause of liberty.—The South would then be a Sicily, and the North a Sardinia. Mr. Lincoln would then be entirely absolved from his slave-hunting, slave-catching and slave-killing pledges, and the South would have to defend slavery with her own guns, and hunt her negroes with her own dogs. In truth, we really wish those brave, fire-eating, cotton-growing States would just now go at once outside the Union and set up for themselves, where they could be got at without disturbing other people, and got away from without encountering other people. Such a consummation was "one devoutly to be wished." But no, cunning dogs, they will smother their rage, and after all the dust they can raise, they will retire within the Union and claim its advantages.

What, then, has been gained to the anti-slavery cause by the election of Mr. Lincoln? Not much, in itself considered, but very much when viewed in the light of its relations and bearings. For fifty years the country has taken the law from the lips of an exacting, haughty and imperious slave oligarchy. The masters of slaves have been masters of the Republic. Their authority was almost undisputed, and their power irresistible. They were the President makers of the Republic, and no aspirant dared to hope for success against their frown. Lincoln's election has vitiated their authority, and broken their power. It has taught the North its strength, and shown the South its weakness. More important still, it has demonstrated the possibility of electing, if not an Abolitionist, at least an *anti-slavery reputation* to the Presidency of the United States. The years are few since it was thought possible that the Northern people could be wrought up to the exercise of such startling courage. Hitherto the threat of disunion has been as potent over the politicians of the North, as the cat-o'-nine-tails is over the backs of the slaves. Mr. Lincoln's election breaks this enchantment, dispels this terrible night mare, and awakes the nation to the consciousness of new powers, and the possibility of a higher destiny than the perpetual bondage to an ignoble fear.

Another probable effect will be to extinguish the reviving fires of the accursed foreign slave trade, which for a year or two have been kindled all along the Southern coast of the Union. The Republican party is under no necessity to pass laws on this subject. It has only to enforce and execute the laws already on the statute book. The moral influence of such prompt, complete and unflinching execution of the laws, will be great, not only in arresting the specific evil, but in arresting the tide of popular demoralization with which the successful prosecution of the horrid trade in naked men and women was overspreading the country. To this duty the Republican party will be prompted, not only by the conscience of the North, but by what perhaps will be more controlling party interests.

It may also be conceded that the election of Lincoln and Hamlin, notwithstanding the admission of the former that the South is entitled to an efficient Fugitive Slave Law, will render the practice of recapturing and returning to slavery persons who have heroically succeeded, or may hereafter succeed in reaching the free States, more unpopular and odious than it would have been had either Douglas, Bell or Breckinridge been elected. Slaves may yet be hunted, caught and carried back to slavery, but the number will be greatly diminished, because of the popular disinclination to execute the cruel and merciless Fugitive Slave Law. Had Lincoln been defeated, the fact would have been construed by slaveholders, and their guilty minions of the country, as strong evidence of the soundness of the North in respect to the alleged duty of hounding down and handing over the panting fugitive to the vengeance of his infuriated master. No argument is needed to prove this gain to the side of freedom.

But chief among the benefits of the election, has been the canvass itself. Notwithstanding the many cowardly disclaimers, and miserable concessions to popular prejudice against the colored people, which Republican orators have felt themselves required, by an intense and greedy desire of success, to make, they have been compelled also to recur to first principles of human liberty, expose the baseless claim of property in man, exhibit the hideous features of slavery, and to unveil, for popular execration, the brutal manners and morals of the guilty slave-masters.—The canvass has sent all over the North most learned and eloquent men to utter the great truth which Abolitionists have for twenty years been earnestly, but unsuccessfully endeavoring to get before the public mind and conscience. We may rejoice in the dissemination of the truth by whomsoever proclaimed, for the truth will bear its own weight, and bring forth its own fruit.

Nevertheless, this very victory threatens and may be the death of the modern Abolition movement, and finally bring back the country to the same, or a worse state, than Benj. Lundy and Wm. Lloyd Garrison found it thirty years ago. The Republican party does not propose to abolish slavery any where, and is decidedly opposed to Abolition agitation. It is not even, by the confession of its President elect, in favor of the repeal of that thrice-accursed and flagrantly unconstitutional Fugitive Slave Bill of 1850. It is plain to see, that once in power, the policy of the party will be only to seem a little less yielding to the demands of slavery than the Democratic or Fusion party, and thus render ineffective and pointless the whole Abolition movement of the North. The safety of our movement will be found only by a return to all the agencies and appliances, such as writing, publishing, organizing, lecturing, holding meetings, with the earnest aim not to prevent the extension of slavery, but to abolish the system altogether. Congress should be at once memorialized for the abolition of slavery in the District of Columbia, and the slave trade between the States. The same zeal, activity, energy and earnestness should be displayed in circulating petitions, as in the earlier stages of the movement. We have the pen, voice and influence of only one man, and that man of the most limited class; but with few or many, in whatever vicissitudes which may surround the cause, now or hereafter, we shall join in no cry, and unite in no demand less than the complete and universal *abolition* of the whole slave system. Slavery shall be destroyed.

25

To Elihu B. Washburne[1]

Springfield, Illinois
December 13, 1860

Private & confidential

Hon. E. B. Washburne

My dear Sir. Your long letter received. Prevent, as far as possible, any of our friends from demoralizing themselves, and our cause, by entertaining propositions for compromise of any sort, on *"slavery extention"* There is no possible compromise upon it, but which puts us under again, and leaves all our work to do over again. Whether it be a Mo. line, or Eli Thayer's Pop. Sov. it is all the same. Let either be done, & immediately filibustering and extending slavery recommences. On that point hold firm, as with a chain of steel. Yours as ever

A. LINCOLN

---

[1] Signed autograph letter, owned by Clarke Washburne, Winnetka, Illinois, in *Collected Works*, IV, p. 151.

26

To Henry J. Raymond [1]

Springfield, Illinois
December 18, 1860

Confidential

Hon. H. J. Raymond
My dear Sir

Yours of the 14th. is received. What a very mad-man your correspondent, Smedes is. Mr. Lincoln is not pledged to the ultimate extinctinction [*sic*] of slavery; does not hold the black man to be the equal of the white, unqualifiedly as Mr. S. states it; and never did stigmatize their white people as immoral & unchristian; and Mr. S. can not prove one of his assertions true.

. . . .

. . . . Yours truly
A. LINCOLN

[1] Signed autograph letter, photocopy in the collections of the Abraham Lincoln Association, Springfield, Illinois, in *Collected Works,* IV, p. 156. Raymond sent Lincoln a letter from William C. Smedes, a member of the Mississippi legislature.

27

To William H. Seward [1]

Springfield, Illinois
February 1, 1861

Private & confidential.

Hon. W. H. Seward

My dear Sir On the 21st. ult. Hon. W. Kellogg, a Republican M.C. of this state whom you probably know, was here, in a good deal of anxiety, seeking to ascertain to what extent I would be consenting for our friends to go in the way of compromise on the now vexed question. . . .

I say now, . . . as I have all the while said, that on the territorial question—that is, the question of extending slavery under the national auspices,—I am inflexible. I am for no compromise which *assists* or *permits* the extension of the institution on soil owned by the nation. And any trick by which the nation is to acquire territory, and then allow some local authority to spread slavery over it, is as obnoxious as any other.

I take it that to effect some such result as this, and to put us again on the high-road to a slave empire is the object of all these proposed compromises. I am against it.

As to fugitive slaves, District of Columbia, slave trade among the slave states, and whatever springs of necessity from the fact that the institution is amongst us, I care but little, so that what is done be comely, and not altogether outrageous. Nor do I care much about New-Mexico, if further extension were hedged against. [2]

Yours very truly

A. LINCOLN—

---

[1] Signed autograph letter, Fred L. Emerson Foundation, Auburn, New York, in *Collected Works,* IV, p. 183.

[2] A compromise plan brought forward by Charles Francis Adams and Henry Winter Davis would have allowed for the immediate admission of New Mexico, with or without slavery, leaving the choice to her people. The assumption behind the plan was that although New Mexico would be admitted as a slave state, slavery would not long survive in that climate. Seward apparently participated in drafting this proposal.

28

To John C. Frémont[1]

Washington D.C.
September 2, 1861

Private and confidential.

Major General Fremont:

My dear Sir: Two points in your proclamation of August 30th give me some anxiety. . . .

. . . I think there is great danger that the closing paragraph, in relation to the confiscation of property, and the liberating slaves of traiterous owners, will alarm our Southern Union friends, and turn them against us—perhaps ruin our rather fair prospect for Kentucky. Allow me therefore to ask, that you will as of your own motion, modify that paragraph so as to conform to the *first* and *fourth* sections of the act of Congress, entitled, "An act to confiscate property used for insurrectionary purposes," approved August, 6th, 1861, and a copy of which act I herewith send you.[2] This letter is written in a spirit of caution and not of censure.

I send it by a special messenger, in order that it may certainly and speedily reach you. Yours very truly   A. LINCOLN

---

[1] Copy, written by John G. Nicolay and endorsed in Lincoln's handwriting, in the Robert Todd Lincoln Collection, Library of Congress, in *Collected Works,* IV, p. 506.

[2] On August 30, Frémont had issued a proclamation confiscating the property of all those in Missouri who had taken up arms against the government and confiscating their slaves. The Act of August 6 authorized the confiscation of property used in aid of the insurrection, but only after customary judicial process.

29

To Orville H. Browning[1]

Executive Mansion, Washington
September 22, 1861

Private & confidential.

Hon. O. H. Browning
My dear Sir

Yours of the 17th is just received; and coming from you, I confess it astonishes me. That you should object to my adhering to a law, which you had assisted in making, and presenting to me, less than a month before, is odd enough. But this is a very small part. Genl. Fremont's proclamation, as to confiscation of property, and the liberation of slaves, is *purely political,* and not within the range of *military* law, or necessity. If a commanding General finds a necessity to seize the farm of a private owner, for a pasture, an encampment, or a fortification, he has the right to do so, and to so hold it, as long as the necessity lasts; and this is within military law, because within military necessity. But to say the farm shall no longer belong to the owner, or his heirs forever; and this as well when the farm is not needed for military purposes as when it is, is purely political, without the savor of military law about it. And the same is true of slaves. If the General needs them, he can seize them, and use them; but when the need is past, it is not for him to fix their permanent future condition. That must be settled according to laws made by law-makers, and not by military proclamations. The proclamation in the point in question, is simply "dictatorship." It assumes that the general may do *anything* he pleases —confiscate the lands and free the slaves of *loyal* people, as well as of disloyal ones. And going the whole figure I have no doubt would be more popular with some thoughtless people, than that which has been

---

[1] Signed letter, Illinois State Historical Library, Springfield, Illinois, in *Collected Works,* IV, pp. 531–533. Browning, a Republican Senator from Illinois, was a friend of Lincoln's.

---

done! But I cannot assume this reckless position; nor allow others to assume it on my responsibility. You speak of it as being the only means of *saving* the government. On the contrary it is itself the surrender of the government. Can it be pretended that it is any longer the government of the U.S.—any government of Constitution and laws,—wherein a General, or a President, may make permanent rules of property by proclamation?

I do not say Congress might not with propriety pass a law, on the point, just such as General Fremont proclaimed. I do not say I might not, as a member of Congress, vote for it. What I object to, is, that I as President, shall expressly or impliedly seize and exercise the permanent legislative functions of the government.

So much as to principle. Now as to policy. No doubt the thing was popular in some quarters, and would have been more so if it had been a general declaration of emancipation. The Kentucky Legislature would not budge till that proclamation was modified; and Gen. Anderson telegraphed me that on the news of Gen. Fremont having actually issued deeds of manumission, a whole company of our Volunteers threw down their arms and disbanded. I was so assured, as to think it probable, that the very arms we had furnished Kentucky would be turned against us. I think to lose Kentucky is nearly the same as to lose the whole game. Kentucky gone, we can not hold Missouri, nor, as I think, Maryland. These all against us, and the job on our hands is too large for us. We would as well consent to separation at once, including the surrender of this capitol. On the contrary, if you will give up your restlessness for new positions, and back me manfully on the grounds upon which you and other kind friends gave me the election, and have approved in my public documents, we shall go through triumphantly.

•   •   •   •   •

. . . Your friend as ever   A. LINCOLN

30

Annual Message to Congress[1]

December 3, 1861

Fellow Citizens of the Senate and House of Representatives:

. . . . .

Under and by virtue of the act of Congress entitled "An act to confiscate property used for insurrectionary purposes," approved August, 6, 1861, the legal claims of certain persons to the labor and service of certain other persons have become forfeited; and numbers of the latter, thus liberated, are already dependent on the United States, and must be provided for in some way. Besides this, it is not impossible that some of the States will pass similar enactments for their own benefit respectively, and by operation of which persons of the same class will be thrown upon them for disposal. In such case I recommend that Congress provide for accepting such persons from such States, according to some mode of valuation, in lieu, *pro tanto,* of direct taxes, or upon some other plan to be agreed on with such States respectively; that such persons, on such acceptance by the general government, be at once deemed free; and that, in any event, steps be taken for colonizing both classes, (or the one first mentioned, if the other shall not be brought into existence,) at some place, or places, in a climate congenial to them. It might be well to consider, too,— whether the free colored people already in the United States could not, so far as individuals may desire, be included in such colonization.[2]

---

[1] Signed document, National Archives, Washington, D. C., and Senate Executive Document No. 1, Thirty-Seventh Congress, Second Session, in *Collected Works,* V, pp. 48–49.

[2] The colonization of freed blacks was an idea with a long history in the United States. Thomas Jefferson, who was philosophically opposed to slavery, maintained that slavery could only be abolished if the freed Negroes were removed so that they would not come into conflict with whites. Lincoln's political hero, Henry Clay, had been a firm advocate of African colonization for freed

---

To carry out the plan of colonization may involve the acquiring of territory, and also the appropriation of money beyond that to be expended in the territorial acquisition. Having practiced the acquisition of territory for nearly sixty years, the question of constitutional power to do so is no longer an open one with us. The power was questioned at first by Mr. Jefferson, who, however, in the purchase of Louisiana, yielded his scruples on the plea of great expediency. If it be said that the only legitimate object of acquiring territory is to furnish homes for white men, this measure effects that object; for the emigration of colored men leaves additional room for white men remaining or coming here. Mr. Jefferson, however, placed the importance of procuring Louisiana more on political and commercial grounds than on providing room for population.

On this whole proposition,—including the appropriation of money with the acquisition of territory, does not the expediency amount to absolute necessity—that, without which the government itself cannot be perpetuated? The war continues. In considering the policy to be adopted for suppressing the insurrection, I have been anxious and careful that the inevitable conflict for this purpose shall not degenerate into a violent and remorseless revolutionary struggle. I have, therefore, in every case, thought it proper to keep the integrity of the Union prominent as the primary object of the contest on our part, leaving all questions which are not of vital military importance to the more deliberate action of the legislature.

.   .   .   .   .

blacks and he was one of the founders of the American Colonization Society. Although this Society had influential support and actually succeeded in establishing a small freedmen's colony in Liberia, the policy of colonization had little real impact before the Civil War. A militant minority of American Negroes, who despaired of finding justice in this country, supported emigration to Africa, but the majority steadfastly rejected any attempt to persuade them to leave what they regarded as their homeland. At the same time, the tremendous cost of a large-scale emigration project had inhibited widespread support for the plan.

31

Fellow-citizens of the Senate, and House of Representatives,

I recommend the adoption of a Joint Resolution by your honorable bodies which shall be substantially as follows:

"Resolved that the United States ought to co-operate with any state which may adopt gradual abolishment of slavery, giving to such state pecuniary aid, to be used by such state in it's discretion, to compensate for the inconveniences public and private, produced by such change of system"

If the proposition contained in the resolution does not meet the approval of Congress and the country, there is the end; but if it does command such approval, I deem it of importance that the states and people immediately interested, should be at once distinctly notified of the fact, so that they may begin to consider whether to accept or reject it. The federal government would find it's highest interest in such a measure, as one of the most efficient means of self-preservation. The leaders of the existing insurrection entertain the hope that this government will ultimately be forced to acknowledge the independence of some part of the disaffected region, and that all the slave states North of such part will then say "the Union, for which we have struggled being already gone, we now choose to go with the Southern section." To deprive them of this hope, substantially ends the rebellion; and the initiation of emancipation completely deprives them of it, as to all the states initiating it. The point is not that *all* the states tolerating slavery would very soon, if at all, initiate emancipation; but that, while the offer is equally made to all, the more Northern shall, by such initiation, make it certain to the more Southern, that in no event, will the former ever join the latter, in their proposed confederacy. I say "initiation" because, in my judgment, gradual, and not sudden emanci-

---

[1] Signed document, National Archives, in *Collected Works,* V, pp. 144–145.

pation, is better for all. In the mere financial, or pecuniary view, any member of Congress, with the census-tables and Treasury-reports before him, can readily see for himself how very soon the current expenditures of this war would purchase, at fair valuation, all the slaves in any named State. Such a proposition, on the part of the general government, sets up no claim of a right, by federal authority, to interfere with slavery within state limits, referring, as it does, the absolute control of the subject, in each case, to the state and it's people, immediately interested. It is proposed as a matter of perfectly free choice with them.

.   .   .   .   .

32

To Horace Greeley[1]

Executive Mansion, Washington
March 24, 1862

Private
Hon. Horace Greeley—
My dear Sir:
   . . . Of course I am anxious to see the policy proposed in the late special message, go forward; but you have advocated it from the first, so that I need to say little to you on the subject. If I were to suggest anything it would be that as the North are already for the measure, we should urge it *persuasively,* and not *menacingly,* upon the South. I am a little uneasy about the abolishment of slavery in this

---

[1] Signed autograph letter, Pierpont Morgan Library, New York City, in *Collected Works,* V, p. 169. Greeley was the editor of the New York *Tribune.*

District, not but I would be glad to see it abolished, but as to the time and manner of doing it. If some one or more of the border-states would move fast, I should greatly prefer it; but if this can not be in a reasonable time, I would like the bill to have the three main features—gradual—compensation—and vote of the people—I do not talk to members of congress on the subject, except when they ask me. . . .

Yours truly

A. LINCOLN

33

Message to Congress[1]

April 16, 1862

Fellow citizens of the Senate, and House of Representatives.

The Act entitled "An Act for the release of certain persons held to service, or labor in the District of Columbia" has this day been approved, and signed.

I have never doubted the constitutional authority of congress to abolish slavery in this District; and I have ever desired to see the national capital freed from the institution in some satisfactory way. Hence there has never been, in my mind, any question upon the subject, except the one of expediency, arising in view of all the circumstances. If there be matters within and about this act, which might have taken a course or shape, more satisfactory to my jud[g]ment, I do not attempt to specify them. I am gratified that the two principles of compensation, and colonization, are both recognized, and practically applied in the act.[2]

. . . . .

---

[1] Signed autograph document, Oliver R. Barrett Collection, Chicago, Illinois, in *Collected Works,* V, p. 192.

[2] Colonization was voluntary. Border state politicians complained that the compensation—$300 per slave—was too low. The act did not require voter approval.

34

Proclamation Revoking
General Hunter's Order of
Military Emancipation of May 9, 1862 [1]

May 19, 1862

By the President of The United States of America.

A Proclamation.

Whereas there appears in the public prints, what purports to be a proclamation, of Major General Hunter, in the words and figures following, towit:

Headquarters Department of the South, ⎱
Hilton Head, S.C., May 9, 1862. ⎰

General Orders No. 11.—The three States of Georgia, Florida and South Carolina, comprising the military department of the south, having deliberately declared themselves no longer under the protection of the United States of America, and having taken up arms against the said United States, it becomes a military necessity to declare them under martial law. This was accordingly done on the 25th day of April, 1862. Slavery and martial law in a free country are altogether incompatible; the persons in these three States—Georgia, Florida and South Carolina—heretofore held as slaves, are therefore declared forever free.   DAVID HUNTER,

(Official)   Major General Commanding.

ED. W. SMITH, Acting Assistant Adjutant General.

And whereas the same is producing some excitement, and misunderstanding: therefore

I, Abraham Lincoln, president of the United States, proclaim and declare, that the government of the United States, had no knowledge, information, or belief, of an intention on the part of General

---

[1] Signed document, National Archives, in *Collected Works,* V, pp. 222–223.

Hunter to issue such a proclamation; nor has it yet, any authentic information that the document is genuine. And further, that neither General Hunter, nor any other commander, or person, has been authorized by the Government of the United States, to make proclamations declaring the slaves of any State free; and that the supposed proclamation, now in question, whether genuine or false, is altogether void, so far as respects such declaration.

I further make known that whether it be competent for me, as Commander-in-Chief of the Army and Navy, to declare the Slaves of any state or states, free, and whether at any time, in any case, it shall have become a necessity indispensable to the maintainance of the government, to exercise such supposed power, are questions which, under my responsibility, I reserve to myself, and which I can not feel justified in leaving to the decision of commanders in the field. These are totally different questions from those of police regulations in armies and camps.

.   .   .   .   .

35

Appeal to Border State Representatives to Favor Compensated Emancipation[1]

July 12, 1862

Gentlemen. After the adjournment of Congress, now very near, I shall have no opportunity of seeing you for several months. Believing that you of the border-states hold more power for good than any other equal number of members, I feel it a duty which I can not justifi-

---

[1] Autograph document, Robert Todd Lincoln Collection, Library of Congress, in *Collected Works,* V, pp. 317–319.

---

ably waive, to make this appeal to you. I intend no reproach or complaint when I assure you that in my opinion, if you all had voted for the resolution in the gradual emancipation message of last March, the war would now be substantially ended. And the plan therein proposed is yet one of the most potent, and swift means of ending it. Let the states which are in rebellion see, definitely and certainly, that, in no event, will the states you represent ever join their proposed Confederacy, and they can not, much longer maintain the contest. But you can not divest them of their hope to ultimately have you with them so long as you show a determination to perpetuate the institution within your own states. Beat them at elections, as you have overwhelmingly done, and, nothing daunted, they still claim you as their own. You and I know what the lever of their power is. Break that lever before their faces, and they can shake you no more forever.

Most of you have treated me with kindness and consideration; and I trust you will not now think I improperly touch what is exclusively your own, when, for the sake of the whole country I ask "Can you, for your states, do better than to take the course I urge? ["] Discarding *punctillio,* and maxims adapted to more manageable times, and looking only to the unprecedentedly stern facts of our case, can you do better in any possible event? You prefer that the constitutional relation of the states to the nation shall be practically restored, without disturbance of the institution; and if this were done, my whole duty, in this respect, under the constitution, and my oath of office, would be performed. But it is not done, and we are trying to accomplish it by war. The incidents of the war can not be avoided. If the war continue long, as it must, if the object be not sooner attained, the institution in your states will be extinguished by mere friction and abrasion—by the mere incidents of the war. It will be gone, and you will have nothing valuable in lieu of it. Much of it's value is gone already. How much better for you, and for your people, to take the step which, at once, shortens the war, and secures substantial compensation for that which is sure to be wholly lost in any other event. How much better to thus save the money which else we sink forever in the war. How much better to do it while we can, lest the war ere long render us pecuniarily unable to do it. How much better for you, as seller, and the nation as buyer, to sell out, and buy out, that without which the war could never have been, than to sink both the thing to be sold, and the price of it, in cutting one another's throats.

I do not speak of emancipation *at once,* but of a *decision* at once to emancipate *gradually.* Room in South America for colonization, can be obtained cheaply, and in abundance; and when numbers shall be large enough to be company and encouragement for one another, the freed people will not be so reluctant to go.

I am pressed with a difficulty not yet mentioned—one which threatens division among those who, united are none too strong. An instance of it is known to you. Gen. Hunter is an honest man. He was, and I hope, still is, my friend. I valued him none the less for his agreeing with me in the general wish that all men everywhere, could be free. He proclaimed all men free within certain states, and I repudiated the proclamation. He expected more good, and less harm from the measure, than I could believe would follow. Yet in repudiating it, I gave dissatisfaction, if not offence, to many whose support the country can not afford to lose. And this is not the end of it. The pressure, in this direction, is still upon me, and is increasing. By conceding what I now ask, you can relieve me, and much more, can relieve the country, in this important point. Upon these considerations I have again begged your attention to the message of March last. Before leaving the Capital, consider and discuss it among yourselves. You are patriots and statesmen; and, as such, I pray you, consider this proposition; and, at the least, commend it to the consideration of your states and people. As you would perpetuate popular government for the best people in the world, I beseech you that you do in no wise omit this. Our common country is in great peril, demanding the loftiest views, and boldest action to bring it speedy relief. Once relieved, it's form of government is saved to the world; it's beloved history, and cherished memories, are vindicated; and it's happy future fully assured, and rendered inconceivably grand. To you, more than to any others, the previlege is given, to assure that happiness, and swell that grandeur, and to link your own names therewith forever.[2]

---

[2] Lincoln read this address to the representatives and senators from the Border States. On July 14, a majority of the group announced their rejection of compensated emancipation for a variety of reasons, including their belief that the plan would not lessen the pressure for "unconstitutional" emancipation by proclamation of Southern slaves.

36

To the Senate and House of Representatives[1]

July 14, 1862

Fellow citizens of the Senate, and House of Representatives

Herewith is the draft of a Bill to compensate any State which may abolish slavery within it's limits, the passage of which, substantially as presented, I respectfully, and earnestly recommend.

July 14. 1862.   ABRAHAM LINCOLN

---

[1] Signed autograph document, New York Avenue Presbyterian Church, Washington, D. C., in *Collected Works*, V, p. 324.

37

Second Confiscation Act[1]

July 17, 1862

CHAP. CXCV.—An Act to suppress Insurrection, to punish Treason and Rebellion, to seize and confiscate the Property of Rebels, and for other purposes.

.   .   .   .   .

---

[1] *Congressional Globe,* Thirty-Seventh Congress, Second Session, Appendix, p. 413.

SEC. 9. *And be it further enacted,* That all slaves of persons who shall hereafter be engaged in rebellion against the Government of the United States, or who shall in any way give aid or comfort thereto, escaping from such persons and taking refuge within the lines of the Army; and all slaves captured from such persons or deserted by them and coming into the control of the Government of the United States; and all slaves of such persons found *on* [or] being within any place occupied by rebel forces and afterwards occupied by the forces of the United States, shall be deemed captives of war, and shall be forever free of their servitude, and not again held as slaves.

SEC. 10. *And be it further enacted,* That no slave escaping into any State, Territory, or the District of Columbia, from any other State, shall be delivered up, or in any way impeded or hindered of his liberty, except for crime, or some offense against the laws, unless the person claiming said fugitive shall first make oath that the person to whom the labor or service of such fugitive is alleged to be due is his lawful owner, and has not borne arms against the United States in the present rebellion, nor in any way given aid and comfort thereto; and no person engaged in the military or naval service of the United States shall, under any pretense whatever, assume to decide on the validity of the claim of any person to the service or labor of any other person, or surrender up any such person to the claimant, on pain of being dismissed from the service.

SEC. 11. *And be it further enacted,* That the President of the United States is authorized to employ as many persons of African descent as he may deem necessary and proper for the suppression of this rebellion, and for this purpose he may organize and use them in such manner as he may judge best for the public welfare.

SEC. 12. *And be it further enacted,* That the President of the United States is hereby authorized to make provision for the transportation, colonization, and settlement, in some tropical country beyond the limits of the United States, of such persons of the African race, made free by the provisions of this act, as may be willing to emigrate, having first obtained the consent of the Government of said country to their protection and settlement within the same, with all the rights and privileges of freemen.

.   .   .   .   .

38

Diary of Salmon P. Chase[1]

Monday, July 21, 1862

．　　．　　．　　．　　．

. . . I received a notice to attend a Cabinet meeting, at 10 o'clock. It has been so long since any consultation has been held that it struck me as a novelty.

I went at the appointed hour, and found that the President had been profoundly concerned at the present aspect of affairs, and had determined to take some definitive steps in respect to military action and slavery. He had prepared several Orders, the first of which contemplated authority to Commanders to subsist their troups in the hostile territory—the second, authority to employ negroes as laborers—the third requiring that both in the case of property taken and of negroes employed, accounts should be kept with such degrees of certainty as would enable compensation to be made in proper cases—another provided for the colonization of negroes in some tropical country.

A good deal of deal of discussion took place upon these points. The first Order was universally approved. The second was approved entirely; and the third, by all except myself. I doubted the expediency of attempting to keep accounts for the benefit of the inhabitants of rebel States. The Colonization project was not much discussed.

．　　．　　．　　．　　．

---

[1] "Diary and Correspondence of Salmon P. Chase," American Historical Association, *Annual Report for the Year 1902,* 2 vols. (Washington, D. C.: Government Printing Office, 1903), II, pp. 45–49, 53–54. Chase was Secretary of the Treasury at this time.

. . . . .

Went to Cabinet at the appointed hour. It was unanimously agreed that the Order in respect to Colonization should be dropped; and the others were adopted unanimously, except that I wished North Carolina included among the States named in the first order.

The question of arming slaves was then brought up and I advocated it warmly. The President was unwilling to adopt this measure, but proposed to issue a proclamation, on the basis of the Confiscation Bill, calling upon the States to return to their allegiance—warning the rebels the provisions of the Act would have full force at the expiration of sixty days—adding, on his own part, a declaration of his intention to renew, at the next session of Congress, his recommendation of compensation to States adopting the gradual abolishment of slavery—and proclaiming the emancipation of all slaves within States remaining in insurrection on the first of January, 1863.

I said that I should give to such a measure my cordial support; but I should prefer that no new expression on the subject of compensation should be made, and I thought that the measure of Emancipation could be much better and more quietly accomplished by allowing Generals to organize and arm the slaves (thus avoiding depredation and massacre on the one hand, and support to the insurrection on the other) and by directing the Commanders of Departments to proclaim emancipation within their Districts as soon as practicable; but I regarded this as so much better than inaction on the subject, that I should give it my entire support.

The President determined to publish the first three Orders forthwith, and to leave the other for some further consideration. The impression left upon my mind by the whole discussion was, that while the President thought that the organization, equipment and arming of negroes, like other soldiers, would be productive of more evil than good, he was not willing that Commanders should, at their discretion, arm, for purely defensive purposes, slaves coming within their lines.

. . . . .

. . . I received a summons to a Cabinet meeting. . . .

There was a good deal of conversation on the connection of the Slavery question with the rebellion. I expressed my conviction for the tenth or twentieth time, that the time for the suppression of the rebellion without interference with slavery had passed; that it was possible, probably, at the outset, by striking the insurrectionists wherever found, strongly and decisively; but we had elected to act on the principles of a civil war, in which the whole population of every seceding state was engaged against the Federal Government, instead of treating the active secessionists as insurgents and exerting our utmost energies for their arrest and punishment;—that the bitternesses of the conflict had now substantially united the white population of the rebel states against us;—that the loyal whites remaining, if they would not prefer the Union without Slavery, certainly would not prefer Slavery to the Union; that the blacks were really the only loyal population worth counting; and that, in the Gulf States at least, their right to Freedom ought to be at once recognized, while, in the Border States, the President's plan of Emancipation might be made the basis of the necessary measures for their ultimate enfranchisement;—that the practical mode of effecting this seemed to me quite simple;—that the President had already spoken of the importance of making of the freed blacks on the Mississippi, below Tennessee, a safeguard to the navigation of the river;—that Mitchell, with a few thousand soldiers, could take Vicksburgh;—assure the blacks freedom on condition of loyalty; organize the best of them in companies, regiments etc. and provide, as far as practicable for the cultivation of the plantations by the rest;—that Butler should signify to the slaveholders of Louisiana that they must recognize the freedom of their workpeople by paying them wages;— and that Hunter should do the same thing in South-Carolina.

Mr. Seward expressed himself as in favor of any measures likely to accomplish the results I contemplated, which could be carried into effect without Proclamations; and the President said he was pretty well cured of objections to any measure except want of adaptedness to put down the rebellion; but did not seem satisfied that the time had come for the adoption of such a plan as I proposed.

.　　.　　.　　.　　.

39

Remarks to Deputation of Western Gentlemen[1]

August 4, 1862

A deputation of Western gentlemen waited upon the President this morning to offer two colored regiments from the State of Indiana. Two members of Congress were of the party. The President received them courteously, but stated to them that he was not prepared to go the length of enlisting negroes as soldiers. He would employ all colored men offered as laborers, but would not promise to make soldiers of them.

The deputation came away satisfied that it is the determination of the Government not to arm negroes unless some new and more pressing emergency arises. The President argued that the nation could not afford to lose Kentucky at this crisis, and gave it as his opinion that to arm the negroes would turn 50,000 bayonets from the loyal Border States against us that were for us.

Upon the policy of using negroes as laborers, the confiscation of Rebel property, and the feeding the National troops upon the granaries of the enemy, the President said there was no division of senti-

---

[1] New York *Tribune,* August 5, 1862, in *Collected Works,* V, pp. 356–357. Members of the deputation have not been identified.

ment. He did not explain, however, why it is that the Army of the Potomac and the Army of Virginia carry out this policy so differently. The President promised that the war should be prosecuted with all the rigor he could command, but he could not promise to arm slaves or to attempt slave insurrections in the Rebel States. The recent enactments of Congress on emancipation and confiscation he expects to carry out.

40

Address on Colonization to a Deputation of Negroes[1]

August 14, 1862

This afternoon the President of the United States gave audience to a Committee of colored men at the White House. They were introduced by the Rev. J. Mitchell, Commissioner of Emigration. E. M. Thomas, the Chairman, remarked that they were there by invitation to hear what the Executive had to say to them. Having all been seated, the President, after a few preliminary observations, informed them that a sum of money had been appropriated by Congress, and placed at his disposition for the purpose of aiding the colonization in some country of the people, or a portion of them, of African descent, thereby making it his duty, as it had for a long time been his inclination, to favor that cause; and why, he asked, should the people of your race be colonized, and where? Why should they leave this country? This is, perhaps, the first question for proper consideration. You and we are different races. We have between us a broader difference than exists between almost any other two races. Whether it is right or wrong I need not discuss, but this physical difference is a great disadvantage

---

[1] New York *Tribune,* August 15, 1862, in *Collected Works,* V, pp. 370–375.

to us both, as I think your race suffer very greatly, many of them by living among us, while ours suffer from your presence. In a word we suffer on each side. If this is admitted, it affords a reason at least why we should be separated. You here are freemen I suppose.

A VOICE: Yes, sir.

The President—Perhaps you have long been free, or all your lives. Your race are suffering, in my judgment, the greatest wrong inflicted on any people. But even when you cease to be slaves, you are yet far removed from being placed on an equality with the white race. You are cut off from many of the advantages which the other race enjoy. The aspiration of men is to enjoy equality with the best when free, but on this broad continent, not a single man of your race is made the equal of a single man of ours. Go where you are treated the best, and the ban is still upon you.

I do not propose to discuss this, but to present it as a fact with which we have to deal. I cannot alter it if I would. It is a fact, about which we all think and feel alike, I and you. We look to our condition, owing to the existence of the two races on this continent. I need not recount to you the effects upon white men, growing out of the institution of Slavery. I believe in its general evil effects on the white race. See our present condition—the country engaged in war!—our white men cutting one another's throats, none knowing how far it will extend; and then consider what we know to be the truth. But for your race among us there could not be war, although many men engaged on either side do not care for you one way or the other. Nevertheless, I repeat, without the institution of Slavery and the colored race as a basis, the war could not have an existence.

It is better for us both, therefore, to be separated. I know that there are free men among you, who even if they could better their condition are not as much inclined to go out of the country as those, who being slaves could obtain their freedom on this condition. I suppose one of the principal difficulties in the way of colonization is that the free colored man cannot see that his comfort would be advanced by it. You may believe you can live in Washington or elsewhere in the United States the remainder of your life [as easily], perhaps more so than you can in any foreign country, and hence you may come to the conclusion that you have nothing to do with the idea of going to a foreign country. This is (I speak in no unkind sense) an extremely selfish view of the case.

But you ought to do something to help those who are not so fortunate as yourselves. There is an unwillingness on the part of our people, harsh as it may be, for you free colored people to remain with us. Now, if you could give a start to white people, you would open a wide door for many to be made free. If we deal with those who are not free at the beginning, and whose intellects are clouded by Slavery, we have very poor materials to start with. If intelligent colored men, such as are before me, would move in this matter, much might be accomplished. It is exceedingly important that we have men at the beginning capable of thinking as white men, and not those who have been systematically oppressed.

There is much to encourage you. For the sake of your race you should sacrifice something of your present comfort for the purpose of being as grand in that respect as the white people. It is a cheering thought throughout life that something can be done to ameliorate the condition of those who have been subject to the hard usage of the world. It is difficult to make a man miserable while he feels he is worthy of himself, and claims kindred to the great God who made him. In the American Revolutionary war sacrifices were made by men engaged in it; but they were cheered by the future. Gen. Washington himself endured greater physical hardships than if he had remained a British subject. Yet he was a happy man, because he was engaged in benefiting his race—something for the children of his neighbors, having none of his own.

The colony of Liberia has been in existence a long time. In a certain sense it is a success. The old President of Liberia, Roberts, has just been with me—the first time I ever saw him. He says they have within the bounds of that colony between 300,000 and 400,000 people, or more than in some of our old States, such as Rhode Island or Delaware, or in some of our newer States, and less than in some of our larger ones. They are not all American colonists, or their descendants. Something less than 12,000 have been sent thither from this country. Many of the original settlers have died, yet, like people elsewhere, their offspring outnumber those deceased.

The question is if the colored people are persuaded to go anywhere, why not there? One reason for an unwillingness to do so is that some of you would rather remain within reach of the country of your nativity. I do not know how much attachment you may have toward our race. It does not strike me that you have the greatest reason to love them. But still you are attached to them at all events.

The place I am thinking about having for a colony is in Central America. It is nearer to us than Liberia—not much more than one-fourth as far as Liberia, and within seven days' run by steamers. Unlike Liberia it is on a great line of travel—it is a highway. The country is a very excellent one for any people, and with great natural resources and advantages, and especially because of the similarity of climate with your native land—thus being suited to your physical condition.[2]

The particular place I have in view is to be a great highway from the Atlantic or Caribbean Sea to the Pacific Ocean, and this particular place has all the advantages for a colony. On both sides there are harbors among the finest in the world. Again, there is evidence of very rich coal mines. A certain amount of coal is valuable in any country, and there may be more than enough for the wants of the country. Why I attach so much importance to coal is, it will afford an opportunity to the inhabitants for immediate employment till they get ready to settle permanently in their homes.

If you take colonists where there is no good landing, there is a bad show; and so where there is nothing to cultivate, and of which to make a farm. But if something is started so that you can get your daily bread as soon as you reach there, it is a great advantage. Coal land is the best thing I know of with which to commence an enterprise.

To return, you have been talked to upon this subject, and told that a speculation is intended by gentlemen, who have an interest in the country, including the coal mines. We have been mistaken all our lives if we do not know whites as well as blacks look to their self-interest. Unless among those deficient of intellect everybody you trade with makes something. You meet with these things here as elsewhere.

If such persons have what will be an advantage to them, the question is whether it cannot be made of advantage to you. You are intelligent, and know that success does not as much depend on external help as on self-reliance. Much, therefore, depends upon yourselves. As to the coal mines, I think I see the means available for your self-reliance.

I shall, if I get a sufficient number of you engaged, have provisions made that you shall not be wronged. If you will engage in the enterprise I will spend some of the money intrusted to me. I am not sure you will succeed. The Government may lose the money, but we

---

[2] The area Lincoln had in mind was the Chiriqui region of Central America, near the Isthmus of Panama. The coal deposits later turned out to be worthless and since the area was involved in a border dispute, Lincoln was forced to abandon the project.

---

cannot succeed unless we try; but we think, with care, we can succeed.

The political affairs in Central America are not in quite as satisfactory condition as I wish. There are contending factions in that quarter; but it is true all the factions are agreed alike on the subject of colonization, and want it, and are more generous than we are here. To your colored race they have no objection. Besides, I would endeavor to have you made equals, and have the best assurance that you should be the equals of the best.

The practical thing I want to ascertain is whether I can get a number of able-bodied men, with their wives and children, who are willing to go, when I present evidence of encouragement and protection. Could I get a hundred tolerably intelligent men, with their wives and children, to "cut their own fodder," so to speak? Can I have fifty? If I could find twenty-five able-bodied men, with a mixture of women and children, good things in the family relation, I think I could make a successful commencement.

I want you to let me know whether this can be done or not. This is the practical part of my wish to see you. These are subjects of very great importance, worthy of a month's study, [instead] of a speech delivered in an hour. I ask you then to consider seriously not pertaining to yourselves merely, nor for your race, and ours, for the present time, but as one of the things, if successfully managed, for the good of mankind—not confined to the present generation, but as

"From age to age descends the lay,
        To millions yet to be,
    Till far its echoes roll away,
        Into eternity."

The above is merely given as the substance of the President's remarks.

The Chairman of the delegation briefly replied that "they would hold a consultation and in a short time give an answer." The President said: "Take your full time—no hurry at all."

The delegation then withdrew.

41

Frederick Douglass:
"The President and His Speeches" [1]

September 1862

The President of the United States seems to possess an ever increasing passion for making himself appear silly and ridiculous, if nothing worse. Since the publication of our last number he has been unusually garrulous, characteristically foggy, remarkably illogical and untimely in his utterances, often saying that which nobody wanted to hear, and studiously leaving unsaid about the only things which the country and the times imperatively demand of him. Our garrulous and joking President has favored the country and the world with two speeches, which if delivered by any other than the President of the United States, would attract no more attention than the funny little speeches made in front of the arcade by our friend John Smith, inviting customers to buy his razor strops. . . .

The other and more important communication of the President it appears was delivered in the White House before a committee of colored men assembled by his invitation. In this address Mr. Lincoln assumes the language and arguments of an itinerant Colonization lecturer, showing all his inconsistencies, his pride of race and blood, his contempt for negroes and his canting hypocrisy. How an honest man could creep into such a character as that implied by this address we are not required to show. The argument of Mr. Lincoln is that the difference between the white and black races renders it impossible for them to live together in the same country without detriment to both. Colonization therefore, he holds to be the duty and the interest of the colored people. Mr. Lincoln takes care in urging his colonization scheme to furnish a weapon to all the ignorant and base, who need only the countenance of men in authority to commit all kinds of violence and outrage upon the colored people of the country. Taking advantage of his position and of the prevailing prejudice against them he affirms that their presence in the country is the real first cause of

[1] *Douglass' Monthly,* September 1862, pp. 707–708.

the war, and logically enough, if the premises were sound, assumes the necessity of their removal.

It does not require any great amount of skill to point out the fallacy and expose the unfairness of the assumption, for by this time every man who has an ounce of brain in his head—no matter to which party he may belong, and even Mr. Lincoln himself must know quite well that the mere presence of the colored race never could have provoked this horrid and desolating rebellion. Mr. Lincoln knows that in Mexico, Central America and South America, many distinct races live peaceably together in the enjoyment of equal rights, and that the civil wars which occasionally disturb the peace of those regions never originated in the difference of the races inhabiting them. A horse thief pleading that the existence of the horse is the apology for his theft or a highway man contending that the money in the traveler's pocket is the sole first cause of his robbery are about as much entitled to respect as is the President's reasoning at this point. No, Mr. President, it is not the innocent horse that makes the horse thief, not the traveler's purse that makes the highway robber, and it is not the presence of the negro that causes this foul and unnatural war, but the cruel and brutal cupidity of those who wish to possess horses, money and negroes by means of theft, robbery, and rebellion. Mr. Lincoln further knows or ought to know at least that negro hatred and prejudice of color are neither original nor invincible vices, but merely the offshoots of that root of all crimes and evils—slavery. If the colored people instead of having been stolen and forcibly brought to the United States, had come as free immigrants, like the German and the Irish, never thought of as suitable objects of property; they never would have become the objects of aversion and bitter persecution, nor would there ever have been divulged and propagated the arrogant and malignant nonsense about natural repellancy and the incompatibility of races.

Illogical and unfair as Mr. Lincoln's statements are, they are nevertheless quite in keeping with his whole course from the beginning of his administration up to this day, and confirm the painful conviction that though elected as an anti-slavery man by Republican and Abolition voters, Mr. Lincoln is quite a genuine representative of American prejudice and negro hatred and far more concerned for the preservation of slavery, and the favor of the Border Slave States, than for any sentiment of magnanimity or principle of justice and humanity. This address of his leaves us less ground to hope for anti-slavery action at his hands than any of his previous utterances. Notwithstanding his repeated declarations that he considers slavery an evil, every step of his Presidential career relating to slavery proves him active, decided, and brave for its support, and passive, cowardly, and treacherous to the very cause of liberty to which he owes his election. This speech of the President delivered to a committee of free colored men in the capital explains the animus of his interference with the memorable proclamation of General Fremont. A man who can charge this war to the presence of colored men in this country might be expected to take advantage of any legal technicalities for arresting the cause of Emancipation, and the vigorous prosecution of the war against slaveholding rebels. To these colored people, without power and without influence the President is direct, undisguised, and unhesitating. He says to the colored people: I don't like you, you must clear out of the country. So too in dealing with anti-slavery Generals the President is direct and firm. He is always brave and resolute in his interferences in favor of slavery, remarkably unconcerned about the wishes and opinions of the people of the north; apparently wholly indifferent to the moral sentiment of civilized Europe; but bold and self reliant as he is in the ignominious service of slavery, he is as timid as a sheep when required to live up to a single one of his anti-slavery testimonies. He is scrupulous to the very letter of the law in favor of slavery, and a perfect latitudinarian as to the discharge of his duties under a law favoring freedom. When Congress passed the Confiscation Bill, made the Emancipation of the slaves of rebels the law of the land, authorized the President to arm the slaves which should come within the lines of the Federal army, and thus removed all technical objections, everybody who attached any importance to the President's declarations of scrupulous regard for law, looked at once for a proclamation emancipating the slaves and calling the blacks to arms. But Mr. Lincoln, formerly so strict and zealous in the observance of the most atrocious laws which ever disgraced a country, has not been able yet to muster courage and honesty enough to obey and execute that grand decision of the people. He evaded his obvious duty, and instead of calling the blacks to arms and to liberty he merely authorized the military commanders to use them as laborers, without even promising them their freedom at the end of their term of service to the government, and thus destroyed virtually the very object of the measure. Further when General Halleck issued his odious order No 3, excluding fugitive slaves from our lines, an order than which none could be more serviceable to the slave-holding rebels, since it was a guarantee against the escape of their slaves, Mr. Lincoln was deaf to the outcry and indignation which resounded through the north, and west, and saw no occasion for interference, though that order violated a twice adopted resolution of Congress. When General McClellan employed our men guarding rebel property and even when Gen. Butler committed the outrage paralleled only by the atrocities of the rebels—delivering back into bondage thousands of slaves—Mr. Lincoln again was mute and did not feel induced to interfere in behalf of outraged humanity.

The tone of frankness and benevolence which he assumes in his speech to the colored committee is too thin a mask not to be seen through. The genuine spark of humanity is missing in it, no sincere wish to improve the condition of the oppressed has dictated it. It expresses merely the desire to get rid of them, and reminds one of the politeness with which a man might try to bow out of his house some troublesome creditor or the witness of some old guilt. We might also criticise the style, adopted, so exceedingly plain and coarse threaded as to make the impression that Mr. L. had such a low estimate of the intelligence of his audience, as to think any but the simplest phrases and constructions would be above their power of comprehension. As Mr. Lincoln however in all his writings has manifested a decided awkwardness in the management of the English language, we do not think there is any intention in this respect, but only the incapacity to do better.

42

Horace Greeley:
"The Prayer of Twenty Millions" [1]

August 19, 1862

To ABRAHAM LINCOLN, *President of the U. States:*

DEAR SIR: I do not intrude to tell you—for you must know already—that a great proportion of those who triumphed in your elec-

---

[1] *New-York Daily Tribune,* August 20, 1862. Greeley was not only the editor of a very powerful newspaper, but he had long been active in Republican politics. In another famous editorial, written during the secession crisis, he had urged the nation to allow the South to depart from the Union.

---

tion, and of all who desire the unqualified suppression of the Rebellion now desolating our country, are sorely disappointed and deeply pained by the policy you seem to be pursuing with regard to the slaves of Rebels. I write only to set succinctly and unmistakably before you what we require, what we think we have a right to expect, and of what we complain.

I. We require of you, as the first servant of the Republic, charged especially and preëminently with this duty, that you EXECUTE THE LAWS. Most emphatically do we demand that such laws as have been recently enacted, which therefore may fairly be presumed to embody the *present* will and to be dictated by the *present* needs of the Republic, and which, after due consideration have received your personal sanction, shall by you be carried into full effect, and that you publicly and decisively instruct your subordinates that such laws exist, that they are binding on all functionaries and citizens, and that they are to be obeyed to the letter.

II. We think you are strangely and disastrously remiss in the discharge of your official and imperative duty with regard to the emancipating provisions of the new Confiscation Act. Those provisions were designed to fight Slavery with Liberty. They prescribe that men loyal to the Union, and willing to shed their blood in her behalf, shall no longer be held, with the Nation's consent, in bondage to persistent, malignant traitors, who for twenty years have been plotting and for sixteen months have been fighting to divide and destroy our country. Why these traitors should be treated with tenderness by you, to the prejudice of the dearest rights of loyal men, we cannot conceive.

III. We think you are unduly influenced by the counsels, the representations, the menaces, of certain fossil politicians hailing from the Border Slave States. Knowing well that the heartily, unconditionally loyal portion of the White citizens of those States do not expect nor desire that Slavery shall be upheld to the prejudice of the Union— (for the truth of which we appeal not only to every Republican residing in those States, but to such eminent loyalists as H. Winter Davis, Parson Brownlow, the Union Central Committee of Baltimore, and to *The Nashville Union*)—we ask you to consider that Slavery is everywhere the inciting cause and sustaining base of treason: the most slaveholding sections of Maryland and Delaware being this day, though under the Union flag, in full sympathy with the Rebellion, while the Free-Labor portions of Tennessee and of Texas, though writhing under the bloody heel of Treason, are unconquerably loyal to the Union. . . .

It seems to us the most obvious truth, that whatever strengthens or fortifies Slavery in the Border States strengthens also Treason, and drives home the wedge intended to divide the Union. Had you from the first refused to recognize in those States, as here, any other than unconditional loyalty—that which stands for the Union, whatever may become of Slavery—those States would have been, and would be, far more helpful and less troublesome to the defenders of the Union than they have been, or now are.

IV. We think timid counsels in such a crisis calculated to prove perilous, and probably disastrous. It is the duty of a Government so wantonly, wickedly assailed by Rebellion as ours has been to oppose force to force in a defiant, dauntless spirit. It cannot afford to temporize with traitors nor with semi-traitors. It must not bribe them to behave themselves, nor make them fair promises in the hope of disarming their causeless hostility. . . .

V. We complain that the Union cause has suffered, and is now suffering immensely, from mistaken deference to Rebel Slavery. Had you, Sir, in your Inaugural Address, unmistakably given notice that, in case the Rebellion already commenced were persisted in, and your efforts to preserve the Union and enforce the laws should be resisted by armed force, *you would recognize no loyal person as rightfully held in Slavery by a traitor,* we believe the Rebellion would therein have received a staggering if not fatal blow. . . . Had you then proclaimed that Rebellion would strike the shackles from the slaves of every traitor, the wealthy and the cautious would have been supplied with a powerful inducement to remain loyal. As it was, every coward in the South soon became a traitor from fear; for Loyalty was perilous, while Treason seemed comparatively safe. . . .

VI. We complain that the Confiscation Act which you approved is habitually disregarded by your Generals, and that no word of rebuke for them from you has yet reached the public ear. Fremont's Proclamation and Hunter's Order favoring Emancipation were promptly annulled by you; while Halleck's No. 3, forbidding fugitives from Slavery to Rebels to come within his lines—an order as unmilitary as inhuman, and which received the hearty approbation of every traitor in America—with scores of like tendency, have never provoked even your remonstrance. We complain that the officers of your Armies have habitually repelled rather than invited the approach of slaves who would have gladly taken the risks of escaping from their Rebel masters to our camps, bringing intelligence often of inestimable value to the Union cause. We complain that those who *have* thus escaped to us, avowing a willingness to do for us whatever might be required, have been brutally and madly repulsed, and often surrendered to be scourged, maimed and tortured by the ruffian traitors, who pretend to own them. . . .

.   .   .   .   .

VIII. On the face of this wide earth, Mr. President, there is not one disinterested, determined, intelligent champion of the Union cause who does not feel that all attempts to put down the Rebellion and at the same time uphold its inciting cause are preposterous and futile— that the Rebellion, if crushed out tomorrow, would be renewed within a year if Slavery were left in full vigor—that Army officers who remain to this day devoted to Slavery can at best be but half-way loyal to the Union—and that every hour of deference to Slavery is an hour of added and deepened peril to the Union. I appeal to the testimony of your Embassadors in Europe. It is freely at your service, not at mine. Ask them to tell you candidly whether the seeming subserviency of your policy to the slaveholding, slavery-upholding interest, is not the perplexity, the despair of statesmen of all parties, and be admonished by the general answer!

IX. I close as I began with the statement that what an immense majority of the Loyal Millions of your countrymen require of you is a frank, declared, unqualified, ungrudging execution of the laws of the land, more especially of the Confiscation Act. That Act gives freedom to the slaves of Rebels coming within our lines, or whom those lines may at any time inclose—we ask you to render it due obedience by publicly requiring all your subordinates to recognize and obey it. The Rebels are everywhere using the late anti-negro riots in the North, as they have long used your officers' treatment of negroes in the South, to convince the slaves that they have nothing to hope from a Union success—that we mean in that case to sell them into a bitterer bondage to defray the cost of the war. Let them impress this as a truth on the great mass of their ignorant and credulous bondmen, and the Union will never be restored—never. We cannot conquer Ten Millions of People united in solid phalanx against us, powerfully aided by Northern sympathizers and European allies. We must have scouts, guides, spies, cooks, teamsters, diggers and choppers from the Blacks of the South, whether we allow them to fight for us or not, or we shall be baffled and repelled. As one of the millions who would gladly have avoided this struggle at any sacrifice but that of Principle and Honor, but who now feel that the triumph of the Union is indispensable not only to the existence of our country but to the well-being of mankind, I entreat you to render a hearty and unequivocal obedience to the law of the land.

Yours, HORACE GREELEY.

New-York, August 19, 1862.

43

To Horace Greeley[1]

Executive Mansion, Washington
August 22, 1862

Hon. Horace Greely:

Dear Sir

I have just read yours of the 19th. addressed to myself through the New-York Tribune. . . .

As to the policy I "seem to be pursuing" as you say, I have not meant to leave any one in doubt.

I would save the Union. I would save it the shortest way under the Constitution. The sooner the national authority can be restored; the nearer the Union will be "the Union as it was." If there be those who would not save the Union, unless they could at the same time *save* slavery, I do not agree with them. If there be those who would not save the Union unless they could at the same time *destroy* slavery, I do not agree with them. My paramount object in this struggle *is* to save the Union, and is *not* either to save or to destroy slavery. If I could save the Union without freeing *any* slave I would do it, and if I

[1] Signed autograph letter, Wadsworth Atheneum, Hartford, Connecticut, in *Collected Works,* V, pp. 388–389.

could save it by freeing *all* the slaves I would do it; and if I could save it by freeing some and leaving others alone I would also do that. What I do about slavery, and the colored race, I do because I believe it helps to save the Union; and what I forbear, I forbear because I do *not* believe it would help to save the Union. I shall do *less* whenever I shall believe what I am doing hurts the cause, and I shall do *more* whenever I shall believe doing more will help the cause. I shall try to correct errors when shown to be errors; and I shall adopt new views so fast as they shall appear to be true views.

I have here stated my purpose according to my view of *official* duty; and I intend no modification of my oft-expressed *personal* wish that all men every where could be free. Yours,

A. LINCOLN

44

Reply to Emancipation Memorial Presented by Chicago Christians of All Denominations[1]

September 13, 1862

. . . . .

"What *good* would a proclamation of emancipation from me do, especially as we are now situated? I do not want to issue a document that the whole world will see must necessarily be inoperative, like the Pope's bull against the comet! Would *my word* free the slaves, when I cannot even enforce the Constitution in the rebel States? Is there a

---

[1] Chicago *Tribune,* September 23, 1862, and *National Intelligencer,* September 26, 1862, in *Collected Works,* V, pp. 419–425.

single court, or magistrate, or individual that would be influenced by it there? And what reason is there to think it would have any greater effect upon the slaves than the late law of Congress, which I approved, and which offers protection and freedom to the slaves of rebel masters who come within our lines? Yet I cannot learn that that law has caused a single slave to come over to us. And suppose they could be induced by a proclamation of freedom from me to throw themselves upon us, *what should we do with them?* How can we feed and care for such a multitude? Gen. Butler wrote me a few days since that he was issuing more rations to the slaves who have rushed to him than to all the white troops under his command. They *eat,* and that is all, though it is true Gen. Butler is feeding the whites also by the thousand; for it nearly amounts to a famine there. If, now, the pressure of the war should call off our forces from New Orleans to defend some other point, what is to prevent the masters from reducing the blacks to slavery again; for I am told that whenever the rebels take any black prisoners, free or slave, they immediately auction them off!

·　　·　　·　　·　　·

"Now, then, tell me, if you please, what possible result of good would follow the issuing of such a proclamation as you desire? Understand, I raise no objections against it on legal or constitutional grounds; for, as commander-in-chief of the army and navy, in time of war, I suppose I have a right to take any measure which may best subdue the enemy. Nor do I urge objections of a moral nature, in view of possible consequences of insurrection and massacre at the South. I view the matter as a practical war measure, to be decided upon according to the advantages or disadvantages it may offer to the suppression of the rebellion."

Thus invited, your delegation very willingly made reply . . .

·　　·　　·　　·　　·

The President rejoined from time to time in about these terms:

"I admit that slavery is the root of the rebellion, or at least its *sine qua non.* The ambition of politicians may have instigated them to act, but they would have been impotent without slavery as their instrument. I will also concede that emancipation would help us in Europe, and convince them that we are incited by something more than ambition. I grant further that it would help *somewhat* at the

North, though not so much, I fear, as you and those you represent imagine. Still, some additional strength would be added in that way to the war. And then unquestionably it would weaken the rebels by drawing off their laborers, which is of great importance. But I am not so sure we could do much with the blacks. If we were to arm them, I fear that in a few weeks the arms would be in the hands of the rebels; and indeed thus far we have not had arms enough to equip our white troops. I will mention another thing, though it meet only your scorn and contempt: There are fifty thousand bayonets in the Union armies from the Border Slave States. It would be a serious matter if, in consequence of a proclamation such as you desire, they should go over to the rebels. I do not think they all would—not so many indeed as a year ago, or as six months ago—not so many to-day as yesterday. Every day increases their Union feeling. They are also getting their pride enlisted, and want to beat the rebels. Let me say one thing more: I think you should admit that we already have an important principle to rally and unite the people in the fact that constitutional government is at stake. This is a fundamental idea, going down about as deep as any thing."

We answered that, being fresh from the people, we were naturally more hopeful than himself as to the necessity and probable effect of such a proclamation. . . .

.   .   .   .   .

In bringing our interview to a close, after an hour of earnest and frank discussion, of which the foregoing is a specimen, Mr. Lincoln remarked: "Do not misunderstand me, because I have mentioned these objections. They indicate the difficulties that have thus far prevented my action in some such way as you desire. I have not decided against a proclamation of liberty to the slaves, but hold the matter under advisement. And I can assure you that the subject is on my mind, by day and night, more than any other. Whatever shall appear to be God's will I will do. I trust that, in the freedom with which I have canvassed your views, I have not in any respect injured your feelings."

45

Diary of Salmon P. Chase[1]

Monday, September 22, 1862

To Department about nine. State Department messenger came, with notice to Heads of Departments to meet at 12.—Received sundry callers.—Went to White House.

All the members of the Cabinet were in attendance. There was some general talk; President mentioned that Artemus Ward had sent him his book. Proposed to read a chapter which he thought very funny. Read it, and seemed to enjoy it very much—the Heads also (except Stanton) of course. The chapter was "High handed Outrage at Utica"

The President then took a graver tone and said:—

"Gentlemen: I have, as you are aware, thought a great deal about the relation of this war to Slavery: and you all remember that, several weeks ago, I read to you an Order I had prepared on this subject, which, on account of objections made by some of you, was not issued. Ever since then, my mind has been much occupied with this subject, and I have thought all along that the time for acting on it might very probably come. I think the time has come now. I wish it were a better time. I wish that we were in a better condition. The action of the army against the rebels has not been quite what I should have best liked. But they have been driven out of Maryland, and Pennsylvania is no longer in danger of invasion. When the rebel army was at Frederick, I determined, as soon as it should be driven out of Maryland, to issue a Proclamation of Emancipation such as I thought most likely to be useful. I said nothing to any one; but I made the promise to myself, and (hesitating a little)—to my Maker. The rebel army is now driven out, and I am going to fulfill that promise. I have got you together to hear what I have written down. I do not wish your advice about the main matter—for that I have determined for myself. This I

---

[1] "Diary and Correspondence of Chase," pp. 87–89.

say without intending anything but respect for any one of you. But I already know the views of each on this question. They have been heretofore expressed, and I have considered them as thoroughly and carefully as I can. What I have written is that which my reflections have determined me to say. If there is anything in the expressions I use, or in any other minor matter, which any one of you thinks had best be changed, I shall be glad to receive the suggestions. One other observation I will make. I know very well that many others might, in this matter, as in others, do better than I can; and if I were satisfied that the public confidence was more fully possessed by any one of them than by me, and knew of any Constitutional way in which he could be put in my place, he should have it. I would gladly yield it to him. But though I believe that I have not so much of the confidence of the people as I had some time since, I do not know that, all things considered, any other person has more; and, however this may be, there is no way in which I can have any other man put where I am. I am here. I must do the best I can, and bear the responsibility of taking the course which I feel I ought to take."

The President then proceeded to read his Emancipation Proclamation, making remarks on the several parts as he went on, and showing that he had fully considered the whole subject, in all the lights under which it had been presented to him.

After he had closed, Gov. Seward said: "The general question having been decided, nothing can be said further about that. Would it not, however, make the Proclamation more clear and decided, to leave out all reference to the act being sustained during the incumbency of the present President; and not merely say that the Government 'recognizes,' but that it will maintain the freedom it proclaims?"

I followed, saying: "What you have said, Mr. President, fully satisfies me that you have given to every proposition which has been made, a kind and candid consideration. And you have now expressed the conclusion to which you have arrived, clearly and distinctly. This it was your right, and under your oath of office your duty, to do. The Proclamation does not, indeed, mark out exactly the course I should myself prefer. But I am ready to take it just as it is written, and to stand by it with all my heart. I think, however, the suggestions of Gov. Seward very judicious, and shall be glad to have them adopted."

The President then asked us severally our opinions as to the modifications proposed, saying that he did not care much about the phrases he had used. Everyone favored the modification and it was adopted. Gov. Seward then proposed that in the passage relating to colonization, some language should be introduced to show that the colonization proposed was to be only with the consent of the colonists, and the consent of the States in which colonies might be attempted. This, too, was agreed to; and no other modification was proposed. Mr. Blair then said that the question having been decided, he would make no objection to issueing the Proclamation; but he would ask to have his paper, presented some days since, against the policy, filed with the Proclamation. The President consented to this readily. And then Mr. Blair went on to say that he was afraid of the influence of the Proclamation on the Border States and on the Army, and stated at some length the grounds of his apprehensions. He disclaimed most expressly, however, all objection to Emancipation per se, saying he had always been personally in favor of it—always ready for immediate Emancipation in the midst of Slave States, rather than submit to the perpetuation of the system.

.　　.　　.　　.　　.

46

Preliminary Emancipation Proclamation[1]

September 22, 1862

By the President of the
United States of America
A Proclamation.

I, Abraham Lincoln, President of the United States of America, and Commander-in-chief of the Army and Navy thereof, do hereby

[1] Signed autograph document, New York State Library, Albany, New York, in *Collected Works,* V, pp. 433–436.

proclaim and declare that hereafter, as heretofore, the war will be prosecuted for the object of practically restoring the constitutional relation between the United States, and each of the states, and the people thereof, in which states that relation is, or may be suspended, or disturbed.

That it is my purpose, upon the next meeting of Congress to again recommend the adoption of a practical measure tendering pecuniary aid to the free acceptance or rejection of all slave-states, so called, the people whereof may not then be in rebellion against the United States, and which states, may then have voluntarily adopted, or thereafter may voluntarily adopt, immediate, or gradual abolishment of slavery within their respective limits; and that the effort to colonize persons of African descent, with their consent, upon this continent, or elsewhere, with the previously obtained consent of the Governments existing there, will be continued.

That on the first day of January in the year of our Lord, one thousand eight hundred and sixty-three, all persons held as slaves within any state, or designated part of a state, the people whereof shall then be in rebellion against the United States shall be then, thenceforward, and forever free; and the executive government of the United States, including the military and naval authority thereof, will recognize and maintain the freedom of such persons, and will do no act or acts to repress such persons, or any of them, in any efforts they may make for their actual freedom.

That the executive will, on the first day of January aforesaid, by proclamation, designate the States, and parts of states, if any, in which the people thereof respectively, shall then be in rebellion against the United States; and the fact that any state, or the people thereof shall, on that day be, in good faith represented in the Congress of the United States, by members chosen thereto, at elections wherein a majority of the qualified voters of such state shall have participated, shall, in the absence of strong countervailing testimony, be deemed conclusive evidence that such state and the people thereof, are not then in rebellion against the United States.

That attention is hereby called to an act of Congress entitled "An act to make an additional Article of War" approved March 13, 1862, and which act is in the words and figure following:

Be it enacted by the Senate and House of Representatives of the United States of America in Congress assembled, That hereafter the following shall be promulgated as an additional article of war for the government of the army of the United States, and shall be obeyed and observed as such:

Article—. All officers or persons in the military or naval service of the United States are prohibited from employing any of the forces under their respective commands for the purpose of returning fugitives from service or labor, who may have escaped from any persons to whom such service or labor is claimed to be due, and any officer who shall be found guilty by a court-martial of violating this article shall be dismissed from the service.

SEC. 2. *And be it further enacted,* That this act shall take effect from and after its passage.

Also to the ninth and tenth sections of an act entitled "An Act to suppress Insurrection, to punish Treason and Rebellion, to seize and confiscate property of rebels, and for other purposes," approved July 17, 1862, . . .[2]

.   .   .   .   .

And I do hereby enjoin upon and order all persons engaged in the military and naval service of the United States to observe, obey, and enforce, within their respective spheres of service, the act, and sections above recited.

And the executive will in due time recommend that all citizens of the United States who shall have remained loyal thereto throughout the rebellion, shall (upon the restoration of the constitutional relation between the United States, and their respective states, and people, if that relation shall have been suspended or disturbed) be compensated for all losses by acts of the United States, including the loss of slaves.

In witness whereof, I have hereunto set my hand, and
L.S.   caused the seal of the United States to be affixed.

Done at the City of Washington, this twenty second day of September, in the year of our Lord, one thousand eight hundred and sixty two, and of the Independence of the United States, the eighty seventh.

By the President: ABRAHAM LINCOLN
WILLIAM H. SEWARD, Secretary of State.

---

[2] For the sections of the law quoted by Lincoln, see p. 90.

47

Frederick Douglass: "Emancipation Proclaimed" [1]

October 1862

Common sense, the necessities of the war, to say nothing of the dictates of justice and humanity have at last prevailed. We shout for joy that we live to record this righteous decree. *Abraham Lincoln,* President of the United States, Commander-in-Chief of the army and navy, in his own peculiar cautious, forbearing and hesitating way, slow, but we hope sure, has, while the loyal heart was near breaking with despair, proclaimed and declared: "THAT ON THE FIRST OF JANUARY, IN THE YEAR OF OUR LORD ONE THOUSAND, EIGHT HUNDRED AND SIXTY-THREE, ALL PERSONS HELD AS SLAVES WITHIN ANY STATE OR ANY DESIGNATED PART OF A STATE, THE PEOPLE WHEREOF SHALL THEN BE IN REBELLION AGAINST THE UNITED STATES, SHALL BE THENCEFORWARD AND FOREVER FREE." "Free forever" oh! long enslaved millions, whose cries have so vexed the air and sky, suffer on a few more days in sorrow, the hour of your great deliverance draws nigh! oh! ye millions of free and loyal men who have earnestly sought to free your bleeding country from the dreadful ravages of revolution and anarchy, lift up now your voices with joy and thanksgiving, for with freedom to the slave will come peace and safety to your country. President Lincoln has embraced in this proclamation the law of Congress passed more than six months ago, prohibiting the employment of any part of the army and naval forces of the United States, to return fugitive slaves to their masters commanded all officers of the army and navy to respect and obey its provisions. He has still further declared his intention to urge upon the Legislature of all the slave States not in rebellion the immediate or gradual abolishment of slavery. But read the proclamation for it is the most important of any to which the President of the United States has ever signed his name.

·   ·   ·   ·   ·

[1] *Douglass' Monthly,* October 1862, p. 721.

The careful, and we think, the slothful deliberation which he has observed in reaching this obvious policy, is a guarantee against retractation. But even if the temper and spirit of the President himself were other than what they are, events greater than the President, events which have slowly wrung this proclamation from him may be relied on to carry him forward in the same direction. To look back now would only load him with heavier evils, while diminishing his ability, for overcoming those with which he now has to contend. To recall his proclamation would only increase rebel pride, rebel sense of power and would be hailed as a direct admission of weakness on the part of the Federal Government, while it would cause heaviness of heart and depression of national enthusiasm all over the loyal North and West. No, Abraham Lincoln, will take no step backward. His word has gone out over the country and the world, giving joy and gladness to the friends of freedom and progress wherever those words are read, and he will stand by them, and carry them out to the letter. If he has taught us to confide in nothing else, he has taught us to confide in his word. The want of Constitutional power, the want of military power, the tendency of the measure to intensify Southern hate, and to exasperate the rebels, the tendency to drive from him all that class of Democrats at the North, whose loyalty has been conditioned on his restoring the union as it was, slavery and all, have all been considered, and he has taken his ground notwithstanding. The President, doubtless saw, as we see, that it is not more absurd to talk about restoring the union, without hurting slavery than restoring the union without hurting the rebels. As to exasperating the South, there can be no more in the cup than the cup will hold, and that was full already. The whole situation having been carefully scanned, before Mr. Lincoln could be made to budge an inch, he will now stand his ground. Border State influence, and the influence of half loyal men have been exerted and have done their worst. The end of these two influences is implied in this proclamation. Hereafter, the inspiration as well as the men and the money for carrying on the war will come from the North, and not from half loyal border States.

.   .   .   .   .

48

Annual Message to Congress[1]

December 1, 1862

Fellow-citizens of the Senate and House of Representatives:

. . . . .

Our national strife springs not from our permanent part; not from the land we inhabit; not from our national homestead. There is no possible severing of this, but would multiply, and not mitigate, evils among us. In all its adaptations and aptitudes, it demands union, and abhors separation. In fact, it would, ere long, force reunion, however much of blood and treasure the separation might have cost.

Our strife pertains to ourselves—to the passing generations of men; and it can, without convulsion, be hushed forever with the passing of one generation.

In this view, I recommend the adoption of the following resolution and articles amendatory to the Constitution of the United States:

. . . . .

"Article ———.

"Every State, wherein slavery now exists, which shall abolish the same therein, at any time, or times, before the first day of January, in the year of our Lord one thousand and nine hundred, shall receive compensation from the United States . . .

. . . . .

"Article ———.

"All slaves who shall have enjoyed actual freedom by the chances of the war, at any time before the end of the rebellion, shall

---

[1] Signed document, National Archives, in *Collected Works*, V, pp. 529–532, 534–536.

be forever free; but all owners of such, who shall not have been disloyal, shall be compensated for them, at the same rates as is provided
for States adopting abolishment of slavery, but in such way, that no
slave shall be twice accounted for.

"Article ———.

"Congress may appropriate money, and otherwise provide, for
colonizing free colored persons, with their own consent, at any place
or places without the United States."

I beg indulgence to discuss these proposed articles at some
length. Without slavery the rebellion could never have existed; without
slavery it could not continue.

Among the friends of the Union there is great diversity, of sentiment, and of policy, in regard to slavery, and the African race
amongst us. Some would perpetuate slavery; some would abolish it
suddenly, and without compensation; some would abolish it gradually, and with compensation; some would remove the freed people
from us, and some would retain them with us; and there are yet other
minor diversities. Because of these diversities, we waste much strength
in struggles among ourselves. By mutual concession we should harmonize, and act together. This would be compromise; but it would
be compromise among the friends, and not with the enemies of the
Union. These articles are intended to embody a plan of such mutual
concessions. If the plan shall be adopted, it is assumed that emancipation will follow, at least, in several of the States.

As to the first article, the main points are: first, the emancipation; secondly, the length of time for consummating it—thirty-seven
years; and thirdly, the compensation.

The emancipation will be unsatisfactory to the advocates of perpetual slavery; but the length of time should greatly mitigate their
dissatisfaction. The time spares both races from the evils of sudden
derangement—in fact, from the necessity of any derangement—while
most of those whose habitual course of thought will be disturbed by
the measure will have passed away before its consummation. They
will never see it. Another class will hail the prospect of emancipation,
but will deprecate the length of time. They will feel that it gives too
little to the now living slaves. But it really gives them much. It saves
them from the vagrant destitution which must largely attend immediate emancipation in localities where their numbers are very great; and
it gives the inspiring assurance that their posterity shall be free forever. The plan leaves to each State, choosing to act under it, to abolish

slavery now, or at the end of the century, or at any intermediate time, or by degrees, extending over the whole or any part of the period; and it obliges no two states to proceed alike. It also provides for compensation, and generally the mode of making it. This, it would seem, must further mitigate the dissatisfaction of those who favor perpetual slavery, and especially of those who are to receive the compensation. Doubtless some of those who are to pay, and not to receive will object. Yet the measure is both just and economical. In a certain sense the liberation of slaves is the destruction of property—property acquired by descent, or by purchase, the same as any other property. It is no less true for having been often said, that the people of the south are not more responsible for the original introduction of this property, than are the people of the north; and when it is remembered how unhesitatingly we all use cotton and sugar, and share the profits of dealing in them, it may not be quite safe to say, that the south has been more responsible than the north for its continuance. If then, for a common object, this property is to be sacrificed is it not just that it be done at a common charge?

.   .   .   .   .

I cannot make it better known than it already is, that I strongly favor colonization. And yet I wish to say there is an objection urged against free colored persons remaining in the country, which is largely imaginary, if not sometimes malicious.

It is insisted that their presence would injure, and displace white labor and white laborers. If there ever could be a proper time for mere catch arguments, that time surely is not now. In times like the present, men should utter nothing for which they would not willingly be responsible through time and in eternity. Is it true, then, that colored people can displace any more white labor, by being free, than by remaining slaves? If they stay in their old places, they jostle no white laborers; if they leave their old places, they leave them open to white laborers. Logically, there is neither more nor less of it. Emancipation, even without deportation, would probably enhance the wages of white labor, and, very surely, would not reduce them. Thus, the customary amount of labor would still have to be performed; the freed people would surely not do more than their old proportion of it, and very probably, for a time, would do less, leaving an increased part to white laborers, bringing their labor into greater demand, and, consequently, enhancing the wages of it. With deportation, even to a limited extent, enhanced wages to white labor is mathematically certain. Labor is like any other commodity in the market—increase the demand for it, and you increase the price of it. Reduce the supply of black labor, by colonizing the black laborer out of the country, and, by precisely so much, you increase the demand for, and wages of, white labor.

But it is dreaded that the freed people will swarm forth, and cover the whole land? Are they not already in the land? Will liberation make them any more numerous? Equally distributed among the whites of the whole country, and there would be but one colored to seven whites. Could the one, in any way, greatly disturb the seven? There are many communities now, having more than one free colored person, to seven whites; and this, without any apparent consciousness of evil from it. The District of Columbia, and the States of Maryland and Delaware, are all in this condition. The District has more than one free colored to six whites; and yet, in its frequent petitions to Congress, I believe it has never presented the presence of free colored persons as one of its grievances. But why should emancipation south, send the free people north? People, of any color, seldom run, unless there be something to run from. *Heretofore* colored people, to some extent, have fled north from bondage; and *now,* perhaps, from both bondage and destitution. But if gradual emancipation and deportation be adopted, they will have neither to flee from. Their old masters will give them wages at least until new laborers can be procured; and the freed men, in turn, will gladly give their labor for the wages, till new homes can be found for them, in congenial climes, and with people of their own blood and race. This proposition can be trusted on the mutual interests involved. And, in any event, cannot the north decide for itself, whether to receive them?

. . . . .

The plan consisting of these articles is recommended, not but that a restoration of the national authority would be accepted without its adoption.

Nor will the war, nor proceedings under the proclamation of September 22, 1862, be stayed because of the *recommendation* of this plan. Its timely *adoption,* I doubt not, would bring restoration and thereby stay both.

And, notwithstanding this plan, the recommendation that Congress provide by law for compensating any State which may adopt emancipation, before this plan shall have been acted upon, is hereby earnestly renewed. Such would be only an advance part of the plan, and the same arguments apply to both.

This plan is recommended as a means, not in exclusion of, but additional to, all others for restoring and preserving the national authority throughout the Union. . . .

.   .   .   .   .

49

William A. Richardson:
"The President's Message" [1]
(Speech in the House of Representatives)

December 8, 1862

Mr. CHAIRMAN: The annual message recently sent to this House by the President of the United States, is the most remarkable of any that has ever been delivered to Congress. It is remarkable for what it says, and it is still more remarkable for what it omits to say. One half of the twenty-one pages which it covers is devoted to the negro. No page, no sentence, no line, no word, is given to laud or even to mention the bravery, the gallantry, the good conduct of our soldiers in the various bloody battles which have been fought. No sorrow is

---

[1] *Congressional Globe,* Thirty-Seventh Congress, Third Session, Appendix, pp. 39–40. William A. Richardson, a Democrat from Quincy, Illinois, had been born and grew up in Kentucky. He had been active in Illinois state politics before his election to Stephen A. Douglas' seat in the House of Representatives. In 1863, after Douglas' death, Richardson was elected to Douglas' Senate seat.

expressed for the lamented dead. No allusion is made to the maimed and wounded. No sympathy is tendered to the sorrowing widow and to the helpless orphan made during the progress of this war, which could have been avoided by honorable compromise, if the President and his friends had chosen so to do.

Sir, it is a remarkable document. It is an extraordinary message, when we come to think of its sum and substance. To feed, clothe, buy, and colonize the negro we are to tax and mortgage the white man and his children. The white race is to be burdened to the earth for the benefit of the black race.

. . . . .

But, Mr. Chairman, there are a few passages in the message so extraordinary, so wonderful, that they require at least a passing notice. There has been, and still is, a great anxiety felt and expressed by our people that this negro population shall not interfere with them; that it shall not jostle them in the occupations they have heretofore pursued in the various industrial pursuits of life in the great fertile regions of the West. The President on that head uses the following language:

"And yet I wish to say there is an objection urged against free colored persons remaining in the country, which is largely imaginary, if not sometimes malicious. It is insisted that their presence would injure and displace white labor and white laborers. If there ever could be a proper time for mere catch arguments, that time surely is not now. In times like the present, men should utter nothing for which they would not willingly be responsible through time and in eternity. Is it true, then, that colored people can displace any more white labor, by being free, than by remaining slaves? If they stay in their old places, they jostle no white laborers; if they leave their old places, they leave them open to white laborers. Logically, there is neither more nor less of it."

Now, sir, I will not do logic the violence to say that that is an argument. He tells our people, those who supported him because they believed he and his party intended to keep the non-slave-holding States and all the Territories of the Union for the sole occupation of the white race, if you do not like my plan of disposing of this black race; if you fear from their introduction among you that their labor will be brought into competition with that of your own, all you have to do to avoid this competition is to quietly leave your present fields of labor, homes to which, perhaps, you may be attached, and the graves of your kindred, and emigrate southward, and occupy the places made vacant by the exodus of what his Excellency terms the "free Americans of African descent." That is the sum and substance of it.

But for sake of argument, admit if you choose that all the plans of the President touching emancipation and colonization of the negro were to-day successfully carried out, what would it accomplish in the great work of restoring the Union? Nothing—worse than nothing.

The President recommends in his annual message three propositions to amend the Constitution of the United States. I will not trouble the committee with reading them; every gentleman here is familiar with the articles he proposes to adopt for amendments. The first, second, and third, are for the benefit of the negro. The people are sick and tired of this eternal talk upon the negro, and they have expressed that disgust unmistakably in the recent elections. The President's proposed amendments as a whole, or either of them, could not receive the suffrages of a majority of the people of more than two States of this Union.

While upon this subject, I desire to call the attention of the committee to a single feature in relation to these amendments. In the message he recommends an amendment to the Constitution as follows:

"Art. —. Congress may appropriate money, and otherwise provide for colonizing free colored persons, with their own consent, at any place or places without the United States."

In this recommendation he seeks to give power to do what he claims he has the power to do without it; and by this recommendation he admits he has been exercising unauthorized and illegal authority. Is not this in itself an admission that the Constitution, unamended, grants no power to Congress or the Executive to appropriate or use the money of the people for any purposes contemplated in this amendment? He calls upon us to compromise. What compromise is that? For whom does he propose a compromise? What for? In order that you may have more power to advance the negro. That is all there is to it, and there is nothing less of it. He tells us there are differences of opinion among the friends of the Union "in regard to slavery and the African race among us." He says to all of those who differ with him, surrender your convictions and come to my plan—and he calls that compromise! Compromise! Yes, I trust in God the day is not far distant when the people of this country will compromise and save the Constitution and the Union for the white people, and not for the black people. Our people are for no other compromise than that.

There are other portions of the message upon which I should like to bestow some attention, but I will forbear to do so now, for I desire to call the attention of the committee to another proposition of the President connected with this subject.

The proclamation of the 22d of September last, issued by the President, took the country by surprise, and no one of the citizens more than myself. I had fondly hoped and been anxious that the President of the United States should so conduct himself in his high office as Chief Magistrate, that I could lend him my support. I have been driven, with thousands of others, into opposition to the policy contained in that proclamation, for reasons which must commend themselves to every reflecting man sincerely desirous of terminating this war and suppressing the rebellion.

Mr. Lincoln, on the 4th of March, 1861, on the east portico of this Capitol, took a vow, which he said was registered in heaven, to support the Constitution of the United States. In his inaugural address delivered on that occasion, he said he had no lawful authority or inclination to interfere with the institution of slavery in the States where it exists. In his proclamation of the 22d of September last, he assumes that he has power to forever free "all persons held as slaves within any State, or designated part of a State, the people whereof shall be in rebellion against the United States," thus violating the pledge so solemnly made in his inaugural address.

If the object of the proclamation was not to aid the rebellion, its effect was. It has strengthened the rebellion by driving into their army every person in the South that it was possible to drive there. Was its intent to affect those alone in rebellion? Clearly not. The slaves of every man in a rebellious State were to be free. The loyal man owning twenty slaves, and the man in the rebel army owning a like number, were, by that proclamation, to be affected precisely the same. The object of the proclamation was to benefit the negro, not to restore the Government or preserve the Constitution. It was nothing more, nothing less. It goes a bow-shot beyond anything done by this House at the last session of Congress.

.   .   .   .   .

50

Speech of James Brooks[1]

December 30, 1862

. . . . .

Gentlemen, . . . we are in the midst of a bloody civil war, the magnitude of which is unlike any thing in the record of human history, except the civil wars of Rome, that drenched the huge Roman Empire in human gore. We, who are not of the Administration, were driven into this war, reluctantly driven in, by the force of unhappy events, and by the then solemn pledge of the Administration, that it was a war, only to maintain the Government and the Constitution of the United States, with the integrity of the Union. (Applause.) We are not now, and we never pretended to be, supporters of the Administration. We drew at first, as we draw now, the constitutional distinction between supporting the Government, and a temporary Administration of that Government. (Applause.) We recognize no loyalty, nor fealty, nor allegiance due to any mere administration of the Government, to no mere man, in no one branch of it—Executive, Legislative, or Judicial—but we do recognize fealty, loyalty, love, devotion, with the whole heart and soul, as due to that great charter of human liberty known as the Constitution of the United States. (Loud and prolonged cheering.) . . .

. . . . .

The magazine so well prepared for explosion during twenty-five years of preparation by extreme men, both North and South, was fired

---

[1] *Speech of the Hon. James Brooks . . . , Papers from the Society for the Diffusion of Political Knowledge,* No. 3 (New York, [1863]), pp. 3–5, 7, 10–11. James Brooks, publisher of the *New York Express,* was a Democrat. His newspaper was identified with the conservative commercial community in New York. The society which published the speech was founded by Samuel F. B. Morse and other Democrats opposed to the Lincoln administration.

at Fort Sumter, and the explosion took place, involving some thirty millions of people in its destruction. The North uprose in mass almost —not to maintain or uphold Abraham Lincoln, or the Cabinet Administration of Abraham Lincoln—but to uphold the Constitution, the three branches of the Government of the United States, its Judiciary as well as its Executive and Legislative authority. (Applause.) "The Constitution *shall* be maintained:" "The Flag *shall* be respected:" "The Union *must* and *shall* be preserved," were the universal rallying cries of the Northern People. (Applause.) The Rebel Enemy authoritatively, through one of its Cabinet officers, (Mr. Walker,) avowed its intent to march upon, and to seize, Washington; —and hence, when the President called for his 75,000 men, more than a million were earnest to volunteer to protect the Capital, to uphold the Flag, to stand by the Constitution. The war then, was solely and avowedly for the maintenance of the Constitution, and the Flag as the symbol of that Constitution.

The Pledge of the Inaugural.

The President himself, in his Inaugural, March 4th, 1861, thus pledged himself against the Abolitionists in his own party, and against his Proclamation of Abolitionism:

> "I have no purpose, *directly* or *indirectly,* to INTERFERE with the institution of slavery in the States where it exists. I believe *I have no lawful right to do so, and I have no intention to do so.*"

.   .   .   .   .

These being the pledges of Mr. Lincoln, . . . now look at the reverse picture, and say, who can, that the whole purpose, the whole *programme* of the war have not been changed? Say, who can, that twenty millions of Northern white men are not now called upon to endure Conscription and Taxation, and to sacrifice themselves in Southern latitudes, mainly to free three or four millions of negroes. (Applause.) . . .

Let me first call attention here to the extraordinary words of the Proclamation [of September 22]. The President speaks of himself, elected but for four years, two of them now nearly expired, as the EXECUTIVE GOVERNMENT OF THE UNITED STATES? Who created

Abraham Lincoln the *Government of the United States?* Who created, who elected him, a man made of no better flesh and blood than the rest of us, to be the GOVERNMENT of thirty millions of people in the United States?

A VOICE—The people. (Cries of "No, no;" "Put him out," "Let him be.")

MR. BROOKS—The people! *Never!* (Exciting cheers.) Never, NEVER did the people give him a majority of their suffrages. (Continued cheers.) He is a minority President, *appointed* by the operations of the Constitution in spite of the people of the United States. (Cheers.) A large majority of the people voted against him, and he was created President in and under that very Constitution he would overthrow by his proclamations. (Great and continued cheers.)

· · · · ·

There is another part of the Proclamation which chalks out, or seems to chalk out, a servile war, which contemplates, or seems to contemplate, the exciting of the slaves to the destruction not only of their masters, but of women and children, and to add the horrors of a servile, thus to the civil war. The words are—

"The Executive Government . . . will recognize and maintain the freedom of such persons (negro slaves) . . . in any effort they may make for their actual freedom."

I do not know that the President means to excite a servile insurrection. I will not impute to him the horrible intent of converting the Southern country into a Hayti or St. Domingo, with the "Authority" of his army and navy to help, but I say, that the language is susceptible of that meaning, and such meaning has been given to it throughout the civilized world. (Applause.) When the "Executive Government" thus addresses negroes or slaves, words ought to be used that negroes or slaves can not pervert into authority to burn, slay, destroy, without regard to condition, age, or sex. (Applause.)

· · · · ·

But, we are told this *Pronunciamiento* against whole States or upon whole States, is, as a matter of mere military policy, or necessity, a wise exercise of the War Power; and it is insinuated that when the negro is thus "pronounced" free on paper, then Sambo, and Scipio and Cæsar will embrace their Rebel masters, and bring them into the ranks of our army, and surrender them as prisoners of war to the utterer of this Paper Proclamation. (Laughter and applause.) We shall see. We shall see. But I deny that there is any wisdom in this Paper as a war measure. I deny that it is a military policy. Its first effect has been to disunite the North, and to raise up a large majority in that North, certainly in the central States of the North, in opposition to this species of Administration. (Applause.) And the next effect has been, while thus disuniting the North, to unite the whole South as one man against a government carrying on a war on such principles. (A voice —"That's so.") We, who were united, have become a *divided* People, and they who were divided, have become a united people;—and if this be military policy, I must say, I don't see it. Do you? (Laughter.) It is a matter of record, too, that since the utterance of this Paper, while Providence before blessed our arms, when fighting for the Constitution and the Laws; now, Providence in a good degree has ceased to smile upon us. . . . The military policy of the President has made popular, South, what was there but an odious conscription, and what the people were preparing to resist. A war, becoming unpopular, has there been made popular; while a war here, at the start popular, is becoming unpopular, because of the false pretenses under which men were engaged or enlisted in it. (Applause.) Hence, I deny that there is any military necessity for this Paper, or that there is any military policy in it. (Cheers.) It is costing us already seas of blood, and will cost us, if thus persisted in, the entailment of a debt upon generation after generation, so that labor, for centuries, will be subjected to capital. (Cheers.)

.   .   .   .   .

But we are told, gentlemen—no matter what Constitution, no matter what the laws of nations, this is a war power President Lincoln is using to support the very life of the nation. He has the right to exert any, and whatsoever power he may deem best fitted to subdue the common enemy. Or, in other words, the President of the United States has but to involve the people in a war, with any body, ostensibly to maintain the Constitution, and he can then pervert that war, to subvert that Constitution, and to extinguish the life of the nation. (Applause.) What proposition more absurd? What better confutation than the mere simple statement of such an absurd proposition. (Applause.) In an abstract struggle, then, for the Republic, we must die in Despotism! To live, we must commit suicide! To restore the Union, we must make the Union not worth a restoration! Now this is not the sort of Government under which we bargained to live, or to die even. (Cries of "no, no.") We have never agreed to subvert the Constitution in order to restore the Union. We have never agreed to surrender Liberty, Property, Free Speech, Free discussion, or Freedom in the concrete or abstract to any Executive Government, or Executive Power. (Cries of Never, never.) And if ever the time comes, when under any "War Power," it may be necessary to subvert the Constitution, and thus to give up our Rights and Liberties, it is a matter of indifference to me, whether a Union thus achieved, be maintained or not; and I say here, and hesitate not to say, that the quicker we be rid of such a Union, under such a Government, the better for all concerned. (Loud, and prolonged, and reiterated applause, the audience rising and giving three cheers for Mr. Brooks.) This War Power is a new name for a very old thing. It is the new name of Despotism, and of Military Despotism, the very worst sort of despotism on earth. . . . He who attempts to govern the People, under any other Power than the Powers of the Constitution; he who leaps over the Laws of Civil Liberty, and the Civil Law, into that boundless field of Despotism, claimed as a War Power, establishes principles and precedents, from Emperors and Cæsars, and merits the execrations of every free man. (Applause.) Hence, I say, when a President ordains Law by Proclamation, under the pretense that he has such right, under any unknown, illimitable War Power, his Proclamation is not to be regarded as Law; it is not Law—(cheers)—and the President of the United States has no more right to declare it Law, than you or I, or any other man. (Tremendous and long-continued cheering.)

.   .   .   .   .

51

Emancipation Proclamation[1]

January 1, 1863

By the President of the United States of America:

A Proclamation.

Whereas, on the twentysecond day of September, in the year of our Lord one thousand eight hundred and sixty two, a proclamation was issued by the President of the United States, . . .

.   .   .   .   .

Now, therefore I, Abraham Lincoln, President of the United States, by virtue of the power in me vested as Commander-in-Chief, of the Army and Navy of the United States in time of actual armed rebellion against authority and government of the United States, and as a fit and necessary war measure for suppressing said rebellion, do, on this first day of January, in the year of our Lord one thousand eight hundred and sixty three, and in accordance with my purpose so to do publicly proclaimed for the full period of one hundred days, from the day first above mentioned, order and designate as the States and parts of States wherein the people thereof respectively, are this day in rebellion against the United States, the following, towit:

Arkansas, Texas, Louisiana, (except the Parishes of St. Bernard, Plaquemines, Jefferson, St. Johns, St. Charles, St. James[,] Ascension, Assumption, Terrebonne, Lafourche, St. Mary, St. Martin, and Orleans, including the city of New-Orleans) Mississippi, Alabama, Florida, Georgia, South-Carolina, North-Carolina, and Virginia, (except the fortyeight counties designated as West Virginia, and also the coun-

---

[1] Photographic copy of the signed autograph document in the Robert Todd Lincoln Collection, Library of Congress, in *Collected Works*, VI, pp. 28–30. The deleted section reprinted the third and fourth paragraphs of the preliminary proclamation.

ties of Berkley, Accomac, Northampton, Elizabeth-City, York, Princess Ann, and Norfolk, including the cities of Norfolk & Portsmouth [)]; and which excepted parts are, for the present, left precisely as if this proclamation were not issued.

And by virtue of the power, and for the purpose aforesaid, I do order and declare that all persons held as slaves within said designated States, and parts of States, are, and henceforward shall be free; and that the Executive government of the United States, including the military and naval authorities thereof, will recognize and maintain the freedom of said persons.

And I hereby enjoin upon the people so declared to be free to abstain from all violence, unless in necessary self-defence; and I recommend to them that, in all cases when allowed, they labor faithfully for reasonable wages.

And I further declare and make known, that such persons of suitable condition, will be received into the armed service of the United States to garrison forts, positions, stations, and other places, and to man vessels of all sorts in said service.

And upon this act, sincerely believed to be an act of justice, warranted by the Constitution, upon military necessity, I invoke the considerate judgment of mankind, and the gracious favor of Almighty God.

In witness whereof, I have hereunto set my hand and caused the seal of the United States to be affixed.

Done at the City of Washington, this first day of January, in the year of our Lord one thousand eight hundred [L.S.] and sixty three, and of the Independence of the United States of America the eighty-seventh.

By the President: ABRAHAM LINCOLN
WILLIAM H. SEWARD, Secretary of State.

52

Frederick Douglass: "The Proclamation and a Negro Army"[1]

February 1863

I congratulate you, upon what may be called the greatest event of our nation's history if not the greatest event of the century. In the eye of the Constitution, the supreme law of the land, there is not now, and there has not been, since the first day of January, a single slave lawfully deprived of Liberty in any of the States now recognized as in Rebellion against the National Government. In all those States Slavery is now in law, as in fact, a system of lawless violence, against which the slave may lawfully defend himself.—[Cheers.] In the hurry and excitement of the moment, it is difficult to grasp the full and complete significance of President Lincoln's proclamation. The change in the attitude of the Government is vast and startling. For more than sixty years the Federal Government has been little better than a stupendous engine of Slavery and oppression, through which Slavery has ruled us, as with a rod of iron.—The boast that Cotton is King was no empty boast. Assuming that our Government and people will sustain the President and his Proclamation, we can scarcely conceive of a more complete revolution in the position of a nation. England, no longer ruled by a king, the Pope turned Protestant, Austria—a Republic, would not present a greater revolution. I hail it as the doom of Slavery in all the States. . . . Color is no longer a crime or a badge of bondage. At last the out-spread wings of the American Eagle afford shelter and protection to men of all colors, all countries, and all climes, and the long oppressed black man may honorably fall or gloriously flourish under the star-spangled banner. [Applause.] I stand here to-night not only as a colored man and an American, but, by the express decision of the Attorney-General of the United States, as a colored citizen, having, in common with all other citizens, a stake in the safety, pros-

---

[1] Speech at the Cooper Institute, February 1863, *Douglass' Monthly*, March 1863, pp. 804–805, 807, 808.

perity, honor, and glory of a common country. [Cheering.] We are all liberated by this proclamation. Everybody is liberated. The white man is liberated, the black man is liberated, the brave men now fighting the battles of their country against rebels and traitors are now liberated, and may strike with all their might, even if they do by thus manfully striking hurt the Rebels, at their most sensitive point.—[Applause.] I congratulate you upon this amazing change—this amazing approximation toward the sacred truth of human liberty.—All the space between man's mind and God's mind, says Parker, is crowded with truths that wait to be discovered and organized into law for the better government of society. Mr. Lincoln has not exactly discovered a new truth, but he has dared, in this dark hour of national peril, to apply an old truth, long ago acknowledged in theory by the nation—a truth which carried the American people safely through the war for independence, and one which will carry us, as I believe, safely through the present terrible and sanguinary conflict for national life, if we shall but faithfully live up to that great truth. [Cheers.]—Born and reared as a slave, as I was, and wearing on my back the marks of the slavedriver's lash, as I do, it is natural that I should value the Emancipation Proclamation for what it is destined to do for the slaves. I do value it for that. It is a mighty event for the bondman, but it is a still mightier event for the nation at large, and mighty as it is for both, the slave and the nation, it is still mightier when viewed in its relation to the cause of truth and justice throughout the world.—It is in this last character that I prefer to consider it. There are certain great national acts, which by their relation to universal principles, properly belong to the whole human family, and Abraham Lincoln's Proclamation of the 1st of January, 1863, is one of these acts. Henceforth that day shall take rank with the Fourth of July. [Applause.] Henceforth it becomes the date of a new and glorious era in the history of American liberty. Henceforth it shall stand associated in the minds of men, with all those stately steps of mankind; from the regions of error and oppression, which have lifted them from the trial by poison and fire to the trial by Jury—from the arbitrary will of a despot to the sacred writ of habeas corpus—from abject serfdom to absolute citizenship. It will stand in the history of civilization with Catholic Emancipation, with the British Reform Bill, with the repeal of Corn Laws and with that noble act of Russian liberty, by which twenty millions of serfs, against the clamors of haughty tyrants, have been released from servitude [Loud cheering.] Aye! It will stand with every distinguished event which marks any advance made by mankind from the thraldom and darkness of error to the glorious liberty of truth, I believe in the millenium—the final perfection of the race, and hail this Proclamation, though wrung out under the goading lash of a stern military necessity, as one reason of the hope that is in me. Men may see in it only a military necessity. To me it has a higher significance. It is a grand moral necessity.

.   .   .   .   .

It is objected to the Proclamation of Freedom, that it only abolishes Slavery in the Rebel States. To me it seems a blunder that Slavery was not declared abolished everywhere in the Republic. Slavery anywhere endangers the National cause, and should perish everywhere. [Loud applause.] But even in this omission of the Proclamation the evil is more seeming than real. When Virginia is a free State, Maryland cannot be a slave State. When Missouri is a free State, Kentucky cannot be a slave State. [Cheers.] Slavery must stand or fall together. Strike it at either extreme—either on the head or at the heel, and it dies. A brick knocked down at either end of the row brings every brick in it to the ground. [Applause.] You have heard the story of the Irishman who paid the price of two spurs—but refused to carry away but one; on the ground, as he said, that if he could make one side of his horse go, he would risk the other. [Laughter and cheering.] So I say, if we can strike down Slavery in the Rebel States, I will risk the downfall of Slavery in the Border States. [Cheering.] It is again objected to this Proclamation that it is only an ink and paper proclamation. I admit it. The objector might go a step further, and assert that there was a time when this Proclamation was only a thought, a sentiment, an idea—a hope of some radical Abolitionist—for such it truly was. But what of it?—The world has never advanced a single inch in the right direction, when the movement could not be traced to some such small beginning. The bill abolishing Slavery, and giving freedom to eight hundred thousand people in the West Indies, was a paper bill.—The Reform bill that broke up the rotten borough system in England, was a paper bill. The act of Catholic Emancipation was a paper act; and so was the bill repealing the Corn Laws. Greater than all, our own Declaration of Independence was at one time but ink and paper. [Cheering.] The freedom of the American colonies date from no particular battle during the war. No man can tell upon what particular day we won our national independence. But the birth of our freedom is fixed on the day of the going forth of the

Declaration of Independence. In like manner aftercoming generations will celebrate the first of January as the day which brought liberty and manhood to the American slaves.—[Loud cheers.] How shall this be done? I answer: That the paper Proclamation must now be made iron, lead and fire, by the prompt employment of the negro's arm in this contest. [Great applause.] I hold that the Proclamation, good as it is, will be worthless—a miserable mockery—unless the nation shall so far conquer its prejudice as to welcome into the army full-grown black men to help fight the battles of the Republic. [Renewed applause.] I know it is said that the negroes won't fight. But I distrust the accuser. In one breath the Copperheads tell you that the slaves won't fight, and in the next they tell you that the only effect of the Proclamation is to make the slaves cut their master's throats [laughter] and stir up insurrections all over the South.—The same men tell you that the negroes are lazy and good for nothing, and in the next breath they tell you that they will all come North and take the labor away from the laboring white men here. [Laughter and cheers.]

. . . . .

You want to know what the colored people think. I will tell you how joyfully they received the Proclamation of Abraham Lincoln. We were not all colored either; but we all seemed to be about of one color that day. We met in good spirits at 10 o'clock expecting before the adjournment to have the Proclamation. We had waited on each speaker keeping our eye on the door.—No Proclamation. The President said we would meet again at two when he had no doubt we should have the Proclamation. We met again but no Proclamation. We did not know whether to shout or hold our peace but we adjourned again with the understanding that it was on the wires and we should certainly see it in the evening. But no Proclamation came. We went on until 11 o'clock and I said, we won't go home till morning. By and by Judge Russell went to one of the newspaper offices and obtained a slip containing the Proclamation. I never saw enthusiasm before. I never saw joy before. Men, women, young and old, were up; hats and bonnets were in the air, and we gave three cheers for Abraham Lincoln and three cheers for almost everybody else. Some prayed and some sang, and finally we adjourned from that place to meet in the Rev. Mr. Grimes' Church. . . . The feeling of the whole of this black Congregation—for it was mainly black—was that they were ready to offer their services at any moment this Government should call for them. And I want to assure you, and the Government, and everybody, that we are ready, and we only ask to be called into this service. What a glorious day when Slavery shall be no more in this country, when we have blotted out this system of wrong, and made this United States in fact and in truth what it is in theory—The land of the Free and the Home of the Brave. [Loud applause.]

FOUR

The Presidency: Emancipation and Reconstruction (1863–1865)

Lincoln had justified his Emancipation Proclamation as the legitimate exercise of his powers as commander-in-chief of the armed forces in wartime, but he knew that there was no guarantee that the courts would sustain his policy when peace returned. Moreover, the Proclamation had not touched slavery in the loyal slave states nor in those areas of the Confederacy that were in Union hands. Many feared (or hoped) that the emancipation policy might still be reversed in an attempt to end the war by compromise. The Proclamation had by no means solved the complex issues involved in slavery and freedom.

As the end of the war was finally in sight, Lincoln faced another pressing problem, how to deal with the seceded states. There was no precedent to guide him and the task of reconstructing the union was complicated by the fact that Congress would also play a role in setting policy for re-admitting the rebel states. Peace-making was further complicated by the savage hatreds that had been roused by the prolonged struggle. Everyone realized that there would have to be some changes before the southern states could be re-admitted to the union; at the very least the leaders of the rebellion would have to be removed from power. But should there be further transformations? For example, should blacks be allowed to vote (blacks were still denied this right in most of the northern states)? Lincoln was struggling with the complex questions of Reconstruction when the assassin's bullet struck him down.

53

To John A. McClernand [1]

Executive Mansion, Washington
January 8, 1863

Major General McClernand

My dear Sir Your interesting communication by the hand of Major Scates is received. I never did ask more, nor ever was willing to accept less, than for all the States, and the people thereof, to take and hold their places, and their rights, in the Union, under the Constitution of the United States. For this alone have I felt authorized to struggle; and I seek neither more nor less now. Still, to use a coarse, but an expressive figure, broken eggs can not be mended. I have issued the emancipation proclamation, and I can not retract it.

After the commencement of hostilities I struggled nearly a year and a half to get along without touching the "institution;" and when finally I conditionally determined to touch it, I gave a hundred days fair notice of my purpose, to all the States and people, within which time they could have turned it wholly aside, by simply again becoming good citizens of the United States. They chose to disregard it, and I made the peremptory proclamation on what appeared to me to be a military necessity. And being made, it must stand. As to the States not included in it, of course they can have their rights in the Union as of old. Even the people of the states included, if they choose, need not to be hurt by it. Let them adopt systems of apprenticeship for the colored people, conforming substantially to the most approved plans of gradual emancipation; and, with the aid they can have from the general government, they may be nearly as well off, in this respect, as if the present trouble had not occurred, and much better off than they can possibly be if the contest continues persistently.

---

[1] Photographic copy of signed autograph letter, Abraham Lincoln Association, in *Collected Works*, VI, pp. 48–49. McClernand, who had served as Congressman from Illinois, had been an outspoken enemy of the abolitionists and a strong proponent of sectional reconciliation.

As to any dread of my having a "purpose to enslave, or exterminate, the whites of the South," I can scarcely believe that such dread exists. It is too absurd. I believe you can be my personal witness that no man is less to be dreaded for undue severity, in any case.

If the friends you mention really wish to have peace upon the old terms, they should act at once. Every day makes the case more difficult. They can so act, with entire safety, so far as I am concerned.

I think you would better not make this letter public; but you may rely confidently on my standing by whatever I have said in it. Please write me if any thing more comes to light. Yours very truly

A. LINCOLN.

54

To Andrew Johnson[1]

Executive Mansion, Washington
March 26, 1863

Private

Hon. Andrew Johnson
My dear Sir:

I am told you have at least *thought* of raising a negro military force. In my opinion the country now needs no specific thing so much as some man of your ability, and position, to go to this work. When I speak of your position, I mean that of an eminent citizen of a slave-state, and himself a slave-holder. The colored population is the great *available* and yet *unavailed* of, force for restoring the Union. The

---

[1] Signed autograph letter, Pierpont Morgan Library, New York, New York, in *Collected Works,* VI, pp. 149–150. Johnson had been appointed as military governor of Tennessee.

bare sight of fifty thousand armed, and drilled black soldiers on the banks of the Mississippi, would end the rebellion at once. And who doubts that we can present that sight, if we but take hold in earnest? If you *have* been thinking of it please do not dismiss the thought. Yours truly   A. LINCOLN

55

To Nathaniel P. Banks[1]

Executive Mansion, Washington
August 5, 1863

My dear General Banks

Being a poor correspondent is the only apology I offer for not having sooner tendered my thanks for your very successful, and very valuable military operations this year. The final stroke in opening the Mississippi never should, and I think never will, be forgotten.

. . . . .

. . . While I very well know what I would be glad for Louisiana to do, it is quite a different thing for me to assume direction of the matter. I would be glad for her to make a new Constitution recognizing the emancipation proclamation, and adopting emancipation in those parts of the state to which the proclamation does not apply. And while she is at it, I think it would not be objectionable for her to adopt some practical system by which the two races could gradually live

---

[1] Signed autograph letter, Illinois State Historical Library, in *Collected Works*, VI, pp. 364–365. General Banks was assigned to command of the Department of the Gulf.

themselves out of their old relation to each other, and both come out better prepared for the new. Education for young blacks should be included in the plan. After all, the power, or element, of "contract" may be sufficient for this probationary period; and, by it's simplicity, and flexibility, may be the better.

As an anti-slavery man I have a motive to desire emancipation, which pro-slavery men do not have; but even they have strong enough reason to thus place themselves again under the shield of the Union; and to thus perpetually hedge against the recurrence of the scenes through which we are now passing.

Gov. Shepley has informed me that Mr. Durant[2] is now taking a registry, with a view to the election of a Constitutional convention in Louisiana. This, to me, appears proper. If such convention were to ask my views, I could present little else than what I now say to you. I think the thing should be pushed forward, so that if possible, it's mature work may reach here by the meeting of Congress.

For my own part I think I shall not, in any event, retract the emancipation proclamation; nor, as executive, ever return to slavery any person who is free by the terms of that proclamation, or by any of the acts of Congress.

If Louisiana shall send members to Congress, their admission to seats will depend, as you know, upon the respective Houses, and not upon the President.

If these views can be of any advantage in giving shape, and impetus, to action there, I shall be glad for you to use them prudently for that object. Of course you will confer with intelligent and trusty citizens of the State, among whom I would suggest Messrs. Flanders, Hahn, and Durant; and to each of whom I now think I may send copies of this letter. Still it is perhaps better to not make the letter generally public. Yours very truly

A. LINCOLN

---

[2] Col. George F. Shepley was military Governor of Louisiana; Thomas J. Durant was a loyalist in New Orleans.

56

To Ulysses S. Grant[1]

Executive Mansion, Washington
August 9, 1863

My dear General Grant:

. . . . .

. . . Gen. Thomas has gone again to the Mississippi Valley, with the view of raising colored troops.[2] I have no reason to doubt that you are doing what you reasonably can upon the same subject. I believe it is a resource which, if vigorously applied now, will soon close the contest. It works doubly, weakening the enemy and strengthening us. We were not fully ripe for it until the river was opened. Now, I think at least a hundred thousand can, and ought to be rapidly organized along it's shores, relieving all the white troops to serve elsewhere.

Mr. Dana understands you as believing that the emancipation proclamation has helped some in your military operations. I am very glad if this is so. . . .

Yours very truly   A. LINCOLN.

---

[1] Signed autograph letter, Chicago Historical Society, Chicago, Illinois, in *Collected Works,* VI, p. 374.

[2] Lincoln and Secretary of War Edwin Stanton sent Adjutant-General Lorenzo Thomas down the Mississippi with plenary authority to enlist and officer Negro regiments.

57

Frederick Douglass:
"The Black Man at the White House" [1]

August 10, 1863

My efforts to secure just and fair treatment for the colored soldiers did not stop at letters and speeches. At the suggestion of my friend, Major Stearns, . . . I was induced to go to Washington and lay the complaints of my people before President Lincoln and the Secretary of War; and to urge upon them such action as should secure to the colored troops then fighting for the country a reasonable degree of fair play. I need not say that at the time I undertook this mission it required much more nerve than a similar one would require now. The distance then between the black man and the white American citizen was immeasurable. I was an ex-slave, identified with a despised race, and yet I was to meet the most exalted person in this great republic. It was altogether an unwelcome duty, and one from which I would gladly have been excused. I could not know what kind of a reception would be accorded me. I might be told to go home and mind my business, and leave such questions as I had come to discuss to be managed by the men wisely chosen by the American people to deal with them. Or I might be refused an interview altogether. Nevertheless, I felt bound to go, and my acquaintance with Senators Charles Sumner, Henry Wilson, Samuel Pomeroy, Secretary Salmon P. Chase, Secretary William H. Seward, and Assistant Secretary of War Charles A. Dana encouraged me to hope at least for a civil reception. My confidence was fully justified in the result. I shall never forget my first interview with this great man. I was accompanied to the executive mansion and introduced to President Lincoln by Senator Pomeroy. The room in which he received visitors was the one now used by the President's secretaries. I entered it with a moderate estimate of my own consequence, and yet there I was to talk with, and even to advise, the head man of a great nation. Happily for me, there was no vain pomp and

---

[1] Frederick Douglass, *Life and Times of Frederick Douglass, Written by Himself* (Hartford, Conn.: Park Publishing Co., 1882), pp. 421–425.

ceremony about him. I was never more quickly or more completely put at ease in the presence of a great man than in that of Abraham Lincoln. He was seated, when I entered, in a low armchair with his feet extended on the floor, surrounded by a large number of documents and several busy secretaries. The room bore the marks of business, and the persons in it, the President included, appeared to be much over-worked and tired. Long lines of care were already deeply written on Mr. Lincoln's brow, and his strong face, full of earnestness, lighted up as soon as my name was mentioned. As I approached and was introduced to him he arose and extended his hand, and bade me welcome. I at once felt myself in the presence of an honest man—one whom I could love, honor, and trust without reserve or doubt. Proceeding to tell him who I was and what I was doing, he promptly, but kindly, stopped me, saying: "I know who you are, Mr. Douglass; Mr. Seward has told me all about you. Sit down. I am glad to see you." I then told him the object of my visit: that I was assisting to raise colored troops; that several months before I had been very successful in getting men to enlist, but that now it was not easy to induce the colored men to enter the service, because there was a feeling among them that the government did not deal fairly with them in several respects. Mr. Lincoln asked me to state particulars. I replied that there were three particulars which I wished to bring to his attention. First, that colored soldiers ought to receive the same wages as those paid to white soldiers. Second, that colored soldiers ought to receive the same protection when taken prisoners, and be exchanged as readily and on the same terms as any other prisoners, and if Jefferson Davis should shoot or hang colored soldiers in cold blood the United States government should retaliate in kind and degree without delay upon Confederate prisoners in its hands. Third, when colored soldiers, seeking "the bubble reputation at the cannon's mouth," performed great and uncommon service on the battlefield, they should be rewarded by distinction and promotion precisely as white soldiers are rewarded for like services.

Mr. Lincoln listened with patience and silence to all I had to say. He was serious and even troubled by what I had said, and by what he had evidently thought himself before upon the same points. He impressed me with the solid gravity of his character by his silent listening not less than by his earnest reply to my words.

He began by saying that the employment of colored troops at all was a great gain to the colored people; that the measure could not have been successfully adopted at the beginning of the war; that the wisdom of making colored men soldiers was still doubted; that their enlistment was a serious offense to popular prejudice; that they had larger motives for being soldiers than white men; that they ought to be willing to enter the service upon any condition; that the fact that they were not to receive the same pay as white soldiers seemed a necessary concession to smooth the way to their employment at all as soldiers, but that ultimately they would receive the same. On the second point, in respect to equal protection, he said the case was more difficult. Retaliation was a terrible remedy, and one which it was very difficult to apply; one which, if once begun, there was no telling where it would end; that if he could get hold of the Confederate soldiers who had been guilty of treating colored soldiers as felons he could easily retaliate, but the thought of hanging men for a crime perpetrated by others was revolting to his feelings. He thought that the rebels themselves would stop such barbarous warfare, and less evil would be done if retaliation were not resorted to; that he had already received information that colored soldiers were being treated as prisoners of war. In all this I saw the tender heart of the man rather than the stern warrior and commander-in-chief of the American army and navy, and, while I could not agree with him, I could but respect his humane spirit.

On the third point he appeared to have less difficulty, though he did not absolutely commit himself. He simply said that he would sign any commission to colored soldiers whom his Secretary of War should commend to him. Though I was not entirely satisfied with his views, I was so well satisfied with the man and with the educating tendency of the conflict that I determined to go on with the recruiting.

From the President I went to see Secretary Stanton. . . . Both the President and Secretary of War assured me that justice would ultimately be done my race, and I gave full faith and credit to their promise. On assuring Mr. Stanton of my willingness to take a commission, he said he would make me assistant adjutant to General Thomas, who was then recruiting and organizing troops in the Mississippi valley. He asked me how soon I could be ready. I told him in two weeks, and that my commission might be sent me to Rochester. For some reason, however, my commission never came. The government, I fear, was still clinging to the idea that positions of honor in the service should be occupied by white men, and that it would not do to inaugurate just then the policy of perfect equality. I wrote to the department for my commission, but was simply told to report to General Thomas. This was so different from what I expected and from what I had been promised that I wrote to Secretary Stanton that I would report to General Thomas on receipt of my commission, but it did not come, and I did not go to the Mississippi valley as I had fondly hoped. I knew too much of camp life and the value of shoulder straps in the army to go into the service without some visible mark of my rank. I have no doubt that Mr. Stanton in the moment of our meeting meant all he said, but thinking the matter over he felt that the time had not then come for a step so radical and aggressive. Meanwhile my three sons were in the service, Lewis and Charles, as already named, in the Massachusetts regiments, and Frederick recruiting colored troops in the Mississippi valley.

58

To James C. Conkling[1]

Executive Mansion, Washington
August 26, 1863

Hon. James C. Conkling
My Dear Sir.

Your letter inviting me to attend a mass-meeting of unconditional Union-men, to be held at the Capital of Illinois, on the 3d day of September, has been received.

It would be very agreeable to me, to thus meet my old friends, at my own home; but I can not, just now, be absent from here, so long as a visit there, would require.

---

[1] Signed letter, Illinois State Historical Library, in *Collected Works,* VI, pp. 406–410. Conkling, an old friend, had asked Lincoln to address a political meeting called to counteract Copperhead influences. The letter was widely printed.

The meeting is to be of all those who maintain unconditional devotion to the Union; and I am sure my old political friends will thank me for tendering, as I do, the nation's gratitude to those other noble men, whom no partizan malice, or partizan hope, can make false to the nation's life.

There are those who are dissatisfied with me. To such I would say: You desire peace; and you blame me that we do not have it. . . .

.   .   .   .   .

But, to be plain, you are dissatisfied with me about the negro. Quite likely there is a difference of opinion between you and myself upon that subject. I certainly wish that all men could be free, while I suppose you do not. Yet I have neither adopted, nor proposed any measure, which is not consistent with even your view, provided you are for the Union. I suggested compensated emancipation; to which you replied you wished not to be taxed to buy negroes. But I had not asked you to be taxed to buy negroes, except in such way, as to save you from greater taxation to save the Union exclusively by other means.

You dislike the emancipation proclamation; and, perhaps, would have it retracted. You say it is unconstitutional—I think differently. I think the constitution invests its commander-in-chief, with the law of war, in time of war. The most that can be said, if so much, is, that slaves are property. Is there—has there ever been—any question that by the law of war, property, both of enemies and friends, may be taken when needed? And is it not needed whenever taking it, helps us, or hurts the enemy? Armies, the world over, destroy enemies' property when they can not use it; and even destroy their own to keep it from the enemy. Civilized belligerents do all in their power to help themselves, or hurt the enemy, except a few things regarded as barbarous or cruel. Among the exceptions are the massacre of vanquished foes, and non-combatants, male and female.

But the proclamation, as law, either is valid, or is not valid. If it is not valid, it needs no retraction. If it is valid, it can not be retracted, any more than the dead can be brought to life. Some of you profess to think its retraction would operate favorably for the Union. Why better *after* the retraction, than *before* the issue? There was more than a year and a half of trial to suppress the rebellion before the proclamation issued, the last one hundred days of which passed under an explicit notice that it was coming, unless averted by those in revolt, returning to their allegiance. The war has certainly progressed as favorably for us, since the issue of the proclamation as before. I know as fully as one can know the opinions of others, that some of the commanders of our armies in the field who have given us our most important successes, believe the emancipation policy, and the use of colored troops, constitute the heaviest blow yet dealt to the rebellion; and that, at least one of those important successes, could not have been achieved when it was, but for the aid of black soldiers. Among the commanders holding these views are some who have never had any affinity with what is called abolitionism, or with republican party politics; but who hold them purely as military opinions. I submit these opinions as being entitled to some weight against the objections, often urged, that emancipation, and arming the blacks, are unwise as military measures, and were not adopted, as such, in good faith.

You say you will not fight to free negroes. Some of them seem willing to fight for you; but, no matter. Fight you, then, exclusively to save the Union. I issued the proclamation on purpose to aid you in saving the Union. Whenever you shall have conquered all resistance to the Union, if I shall urge you to continue fighting, it will be an apt time, then, for you to declare you will not fight to free negroes.

I thought that in your struggle for the Union, to whatever extent the negroes should cease helping the enemy, to that extent it weakened the enemy in his resistance to you. Do you think differently? I thought that whatever negroes can be got to do as soldiers, leaves just so much less for white soldiers to do, in saving the Union. Does it appear otherwise to you? But negroes, like other people, act upon motives. Why should they do any thing for us, if we will do nothing for them? If they stake their lives for us, they must be prompted by the strongest motive—even the promise of freedom. And the promise being made, must be kept.

.   .   .   .   .

Peace does not appear so distant as it did. I hope it will come soon, and come to stay; and so come as to be worth the keeping in all future time. It will then have been proved that, among free men, there can be no successful appeal from the ballot to the bullet; and that they who take such appeal are sure to lose their case, and pay the cost. And then, there will be some black men who can remember that, with silent tongue, and clenched teeth, and steady eye, and well-poised bayonet, they have helped mankind on to this great consummation;

while, I fear, there will be some white ones, unable to forget that, with malignant heart, and deceitful speech, they have strove to hinder it.

Still let us not be over-sanguine of a speedy final triumph. Let us be quite sober. Let us diligently apply the means, never doubting that a just God, in his own good time, will give us the rightful result. Yours very truly   A. LINCOLN.

59

To Salmon P. Chase[1]

Executive Mansion, Washington
September 2, 1863

Hon. S. P. Chase.
My dear Sir:
Knowing your great anxiety that the emancipation proclamation shall now be applied to certain parts of Virginia and Louisiana which were exempted from it last January, I state briefly what appear to me to be difficulties in the way of such a step. The original proclamation has no constitutional or legal justification, except as a military measure. The exemptions were made because the military necessity did not apply to the exempted localities. Nor does that necessity apply to them now any more than it did then. If I take the step must I not do so, without the argument of military necessity, and so, without any

---

[1] Autograph draft, Robert Todd Lincoln Collection, Library of Congress, in *Collected Works,* VI, pp. 428–429. Chase had repeatedly urged Lincoln to apply the policy of the Emancipation Proclamation to those areas of Virginia and Louisiana which had been excluded. Although Lincoln did not send this letter, he read it to Chase on September 17. (*Inside Lincoln's Cabinet: The Civil War Diaries of Salmon P. Chase,* David Donald, ed. [New York: Longmans, Green and Company, 1954], p. 198.)

---

argument, except the one that I think the measure politically expedient, and morally right? Would I not thus give up all footing upon constitution or law? Would I not thus be in the boundless field of absolutism? Could this pass unnoticed, or unresisted? Could it fail to be perceived that without any further stretch, I might do the same in Delaware, Maryland, Kentucky, Tennessee, and Missouri; and even change any law in any state? Would not many of our own friends shrink away appalled? Would it not lose us the elections, and with them, the very cause we seek to advance?

60

Annual Message to Congress[1]

December 8, 1863

.　　.　　.　　.　　.

When Congress assembled a year ago the war had already lasted nearly twenty months, and there had been many conflicts on both land and sea, with varying results.

The rebellion had been pressed back into reduced limits; yet the tone of public feeling and opinion, at home and abroad, was not satisfactory. . . . The preliminary emancipation proclamation, issued in September, was running its assigned period to the beginning of the new year. A month later the final proclamation came, including the announcement that colored men of suitable condition would be received into the war service. The policy of emancipation, and of employing black soldiers, gave to the future a new aspect, about which

[1] Signed document, National Archives, in *Collected Works,* VII, pp. 48–51.

hope, and fear, and doubt contended in uncertain conflict. According to our political system, as a matter of civil administration, the general government had no lawful power to effect emancipation in any State, and for a long time it had been hoped that the rebellion could be suppressed without resorting to it as a military measure. It was all the while deemed possible that the necessity for it might come, and that if it should, the crisis of the contest would then be presented. It came, and as was anticipated, it was followed by dark and doubtful days. Eleven months having now passed, we are permitted to take another review. The rebel borders are pressed still further back, and by the complete opening of the Mississippi the country dominated by the rebellion is divided into distinct parts, with no practical communication between them. Tennessee and Arkansas have been substantially cleared of insurgent control, and influential citizens in each, owners of slaves and advocates of slavery at the beginning of the rebellion, now declare openly for emancipation in their respective States. Of those States not included in the emancipation proclamation, Maryland, and Missouri, neither of which three years ago would tolerate any restraint upon the extension of slavery into new territories, only dispute now as to the best mode of removing it within their own limits.

Of those who were slaves at the beginning of the rebellion, full one hundred thousand are now in the United States military service, about one-half of which number actually bear arms in the ranks; thus giving the double advantage of taking so much labor from the insurgent cause, and supplying the places which otherwise must be filled with so many white men. So far as tested, it is difficult to say they are not as good soldiers as any. No servile insurrection, or tendency to violence or cruelty, has marked the measures of emancipation and arming the blacks. These measures have been much discussed in foreign countries, and contemporary with such discussion the tone of public sentiment there is much improved. At home the same measures have been fully discussed, supported, criticised, and denounced, and the annual elections following are highly encouraging to those whose official duty it is to bear the country through this great trial. Thus we have the new reckoning. The crisis which threatened to divide the friends of the Union is past.

Looking now to the present and future, and with reference to a resumption of the national authority within the States wherein that authority has been suspended, I have thought fit to issue a proclamation, a copy of which is herewith transmitted. On examination of this proclamation it will appear, as is believed, that nothing is attempted beyond what is amply justified by the Constitution. True, the form of an oath is given, but no man is coerced to take it. . . .

> .   .   .   .   .

But if it be proper to require, as a test of admission to the political body, an oath of allegiance to the Constitution of the United States, and to the Union under it, why also to the laws and proclamations in regard to slavery? Those laws and proclamations were enacted and put forth for the purpose of aiding in the suppression of the rebellion. To give them their fullest effect, there had to be a pledge for their maintenance. In my judgment they have aided, and will further aid, the cause for which they were intended. To now abandon them would be not only to relinquish a lever of power, but would also be a cruel and an astounding breach of faith. I may add at this point, that while I remain in my present position I shall not attempt to retract or modify the emancipation proclamation; nor shall I return to slavery any person who is free by the terms of that proclamation, or by any of the acts of Congress. For these and other reasons it is thought best that support of these measures shall be included in the oath; and it is believed the Executive may lawfully claim it in return for pardon and restoration of forfeited rights, which he has clear constitutional power to withhold altogether, or grant upon the terms which he shall deem wisest for the public interest. It should be observed, also, that this part of the oath is subject to the modifying and abrogating power of legislation and supreme judicial decision.

The proposed acquiescence of the national Executive in any reasonable temporary State arrangement for the freed people is made with the view of possibly modifying the confusion and destitution which must, at best, attend all classes by a total revolution of labor throughout whole States. It is hoped that the already deeply afflicted people in those States may be somewhat more ready to give up the cause of their affliction, if, to this extent, this vital matter be left to themselves; while no power of the national Executive to prevent an abuse is abridged by the proposition.

> .   .   .   .   .

61

Proclamation of Amnesty and Reconstruction[1]

December 8, 1863

By the President of the United States of America:

A Proclamation.

.   .   .   .   .

I, Abraham Lincoln, President of the United States, do proclaim, declare, and make known to all persons who have, directly or by implication, participated in the existing rebellion, except as hereinafter excepted, that a full pardon is hereby granted to them and each of them, with restoration of all rights of property, except as to slaves, and in property cases where rights of third parties shall have intervened, and upon the condition that every such person shall take and subscribe an oath, and thenceforward keep and maintain said oath inviolate; and which oath shall be registered for permanent preservation, and shall be of the tenor and effect following, to wit:

"I, ———, do solemnly swear, in presence of Almighty God, that I will henceforth faithfully support, protect and defend the Constitution of the United States, and the union of the States thereunder; and that I will, in like manner, abide by and faithfully support all acts of Congress passed during the existing rebellion with reference to slaves, so long and so far as not repealed, modified or held void by Congress, or by decision of the Supreme Court; and that I will, in like manner, abide by and faithfully support all proclamations of the President made during the existing rebellion having reference to slaves, so long and so far as not modified or declared void by decision of the Supreme Court. So help me God."

.   .   .   .   .

---

[1] Signed document, National Archives, in *Collected Works,* VII, pp. 53–55.

And I do further proclaim, declare, and make known that any provision which may be adopted by such State government in relation to the freed people of such State, which shall recognize and declare their permanent freedom, provide for their education, and which may yet be consistent, as a temporary arrangement, with their present condition as a laboring, landless, and homeless class, will not be objected to by the national Executive. . . .

.   .   .   .   .

62

John R. Eden: "Reconstruction" [1]
(Speech in the House of Representatives)

February 27, 1864

Mr. Chairman, I propose to state some of the reasons why I dissent from the views of the President, as expressed in his recent message, and especially some reasons why I dissent from his plan for the reconstruction of the Union embraced in his proclamation of amnesty.

.   .   .   .   .

This "war power" which is invoked by the Administration and its friends to justify their infringements upon the rights and liberties

---

[1] *Congressional Globe,* Thirty-Eighth Congress, First Session, pp. 858, 863. Like Abraham Lincoln, John R. Eden was born in Kentucky, moved with his family to Indiana, and practiced law in central Illinois. He was elected as a Democrat to the Thirty-Eighth Congress, was defeated when he ran for reelection, but was elected again to the Forty-Third Congress and several times thereafter.

of the people is akin to the "higher law." The "military necessities" of the President and his subordinates, which have formed the pretexts for the various proclamations of emancipation, and for subverting the constitutions and laws of the States and tampering with their elections, spring from the same impure and corrupt fountain. All the powers of this Government are to be found in the Constitution. Military necessity is applicable only to the movements of armies in the field, and does not reach beyond their lines.

The Administration and its adherents seem to be wedded to the peculiar policy they have adopted, and the only way to effect a change is through the agency of the ballot-box. Claiming to be unconditional Union men, the party in power would not accept the Union to-day upon the simple terms of the Constitution, leaving all questions affecting the rights of person and property in the confederate States to be settled by the adjudications of the courts and the future legislation of the country. A fanatical zeal for the freedom of the black man, intensified by a stubborn resistance to every effort to make him free by those whose social and financial ruin would thereby ensue, is turned into a desperate purpose to degrade and enslave the white race whose misfortune it is to be placed among the sable objects of abolition idolatry. These men, who arrogate to themselves all the patriotism and all the religion of the country, would not stop this effusion of blood and arrest the onward course of relentless, cruel war which is now laying waste the fairest portions of our country if every rebel in the land were to lay down his arms and humbly sue for peace. The fiat has gone forth, and as long as a single slave remains in bondage this harvest of death must go on. Regardless of all the lessons of history, in violation of the faith of the nation as pledged by the heroes and statesmen of the past, in open contempt of the solemn promises made to the people in party platforms, presidential messages, and congressional resolves, four million slaves, an inferior and degraded race, whose education and habits wholly unfit them for self-control, are to be thrown upon society to roam at will throughout the land. Yes, and the sword of the nation is to be placed in the hands of this servile race, thus opening their way to the ballot-box and to social equality with the whites. Had such a proposition been made to the American people ere the hearts of so many had become hardened by the severities of this war, no sane man would for a moment have hearkened to it. But, lest some good-meaning people may think that I do my political opponents injustice in what I have said, I will quote from the last annual message of the President. He says:

I may add, at this point, that, while I remain in my present position, I shall not attempt to retract or modify the emancipation proclamation.

In speaking upon the same subject a few sentences preceding what I have read, the President says:

To now abandon them would be not only to relinquish a lever of power, but would also be a cruel and astounding breach of faith.

There are no compunctions of conscience about breaking faith with white men! I charge the President of the United States with breaking faith with the people of this country by disregarding not only his pledges made in the inaugural address, in the proclamation of April 15, 1861, and in the Crittenden resolution, but also by trampling under his feet every provision of the Federal Constitution made for the protection of the liberty of the citizen. All the pledges to the negro are to be faithfully kept. In future the "free Americans of African descent" will doubtless crowd the President's levees, even in greater numbers than they did on New Year's day, not only relieving the monotony occasioned by the uniformity of color, but also giving a foreign *odor* to the gorgeous splendor of American royalty.

Our "freedmen" are the most fortunate people on earth. Even this Administration will keep faith with them. In the amnesty proclamation "our colored fellow-citizens" are treated with the usual affection and tenderness shown them by the President. "All who have engaged in any way in treating colored persons, or white persons in charge of such, otherwise than lawfully as prisoners of war, and which persons may have been found in the United States service as soldiers, seamen, or in any other capacity," are excluded from the benefits of the proclamation of amnesty. The repentant rebel, who may have murdered in cold blood the white soldier thrown into his hands by the fortunes of war, upon taking the prescribed oath is pardoned and taken into the bosom of the Republican party. But the planter within the rebel lines, who has in nowise voluntarily raised his hand against the Government, who attempts to recapture his slave which has been stolen from him and put into the Federal Army, is beyond the reach of executive clemency. He has committed the unpardonable sin. He has laid his profane hands upon what is regarded by this Administration as sacred, and must expiate his crime with his life! The mother who has given up her only son to the defense of the country has the consoling assurance that though the murderer of her boy will be restored to all his rights upon taking the prescribed oath, except the right to own the labor of his servant, yet he who has refused to extend the usages of civilized warfare to the negro shall receive no pardon.

Sir, the liberties of the people, the preservation of the State governments, and the maintenance of the Union under the Federal Constitution, are all involved in the well-defined issues of the approaching presidential election. While there are differences of opinion among Democrats and conservative men upon minor points, some believing that the evils which now afflict the country may be remedied by a vigorous prosecution of the war under the Constitution, and others favoring peace and conciliation as the only means of reuniting the broken fragments of the Union, they all are agreed in a determination to uphold the Federal Constitution and the Union of the States in accordance therewith. Not one would favor negotiations for peace on any other basis than that of a restored Union, with the rights of the States and the liberties of the people guarded and protected by all the limitations of the Constitution upon the powers of the General Government.

The only issue, then, between the parties relative to the war is whether it shall be prosecuted under the present policy for the overthrow of the States, and to compel the entire population of the South to surrender all rights of person and property into the hands of the abolitionists, or whether, under Democratic rule, in case the southern people shall refuse to make peace and return to the Union upon fair and equitable terms under the Constitution, the war shall be waged only against those in hostility to the Government. The policy of the dominant party includes confiscation, emancipation, endless war, despotism. The policy of the Democracy embraces conciliation and compromise, along with whatever force may be necessary to the due execution of the laws, and a firm, unfaltering devotion to constitutional liberty, and a determination as immovable as the everlasting hills to maintain it.

.   .   .   .   .

63

To James S. Wadsworth[1]

January 1864?

You desire to know, in the event of our complete success in the field, the same being followed by a loyal and cheerful submission on the part of the South, if universal amnesty should not be accompanied with universal suffrage.

Now, since you know my private inclinations as to what terms should be granted to the South in the contingency mentioned, I will here add, that if our success should thus be realized, followed by such desired results, I cannot see, if universal amnesty is granted, how, under the circumstances, I can avoid exacting in return universal suffrage, or, at least, suffrage on the basis of intelligence and military service.

How to better the condition of the colored race has long been a study which has attracted my serious and careful attention; hence I think I am clear and decided as to what course I shall pursue in the premises, regarding it a religious duty, as the nation's guardian of these people, who have so heroically vindicated their manhood on the battle-field, where, in assisting to save the life of the Republic, they have demonstrated in blood their right to the ballot, which is but the humane protection of the flag they have so fearlessly defended.

---

[1] New York *Tribune,* September 26, 1865, quoting *The Southern Advocate,* in *Collected Works,* VII, p. 101. No manuscript copy of this letter has been found and the editors of the *Collected Works* have been unable to locate *The Southern Advocate.* Brigadier General Wadsworth, who took an important role in the victory at Gettysburg, had a long record of anti-slavery activities.

64

To James S. Wadsworth[1]

January 1864?

The restoration of the Rebel States to the Union must rest upon the principle of civil and political equality of both races; and it must be sealed by general amnesty.

---

[1] Marquis de Chambrun, "Personal Recollections of Mr. Lincoln," *Scribner's Magazine,* XIII (January 1893), 36. The Marquis identifies this as an excerpt from "a letter he [Lincoln] wrote in 1864 to General Wadsworth." The editors of the *Collected Works* print it as an additional paragraph to the last document; *Collected Works,* VII, p. 102.

65

To John A. J. Creswell[1]

Executive Mansion, Washington
March 7, 1864

Hon. John A. J. Creswell
My dear Sir:
    I am very anxious for emancipation to be effected in Maryland in some substantial form. I think it probable that my expressions of a

---

[1] Signed autograph letter, Robert Todd Lincoln Collection, Library of Congress, in *Collected Works,* VII, pp. 226–227. Creswell was a Republican member of the House of Representatives from Maryland.

preference for *gradual* over *immediate* emancipation, are misunderstood. I had thought the *gradual* would produce less confusion, and destitution, and therefore would be more satisfactory; but if those who are better acquainted with the subject, and are more deeply interested in it, prefer the *immediate,* most certainly I have no objection to their judgment prevailing. My wish is that all who are for emancipation *in any form,* shall co-operate, all treating all respectfully, and all adopting and acting upon the major opinion, when fairly ascertained. What I have dreaded is the danger that by jealousies, rivalries, and consequent ill-blood—driving one another out of meetings and conventions —perchance from the polls—the friends of emancipation themselves may divide, and lose the measure altogether. I wish this letter to not be made public; but no man representing me as I herein represent myself, will be in any danger of contradiction by me. Yours truly

A. LINCOLN.

66

To Michael Hahn[1]

Executive Mansion, Washington
March 13, 1864

Private

Hon. Michael Hahn

My dear Sir:

I congratulate you on having fixed your name in history as the first-free-state Governor of Louisiana. Now you are about to have a Convention which, among other things, will probably define the elec-

---

[1] Signed autograph letter owned by Roger W. Barrett, Chicago, Illinois, in *Collected Works,* VII, p. 243.

tive franchise. I barely suggest for your private consideration, whether some of the colored people may not be let in—as, for instance, the very intelligent, and especially those who have fought gallantly in our ranks. They would probably help, in some trying time to come, to keep the jewel of liberty within the family of freedom. But this is only a suggestion, not to the public, but to you alone. Yours truly

A. LINCOLN

67

To John A. J. Creswell [1]

Executive Mansion, Washington
March 17, 1864

Hon. John A. J. Creswell
My dear Sir:

It needs not to be a secret, that I wish success to emancipation in Maryland. It would aid much to end the rebellion. Hence it is a matter of national consequence, in which every national man, may rightfully feel a deep interest. I sincerely hope the friends of the measure will allow no minor considerations to divide and distract them. Yours truly   A. LINCOLN

---

[1] Facsimile of signed autograph letter, Abraham Lincoln Association, Springfield, Illinois, in *Collected Works,* VII, p. 251.

68

To Albert G. Hodges[1]

Executive Mansion, Washington
April 4, 1864

A. G. Hodges, Esq
Frankfort, Ky.

My dear Sir: You ask me to put in writing the substance of what I verbally said the other day, in your presence, to Governor Bramlette and Senator Dixon. It was about as follows:

"I am naturally anti-slavery. If slavery is not wrong, nothing is wrong. I can not remember when I did not so think, and feel. And yet I have never understood that the Presidency conferred upon me an unrestricted right to act officially upon this judgment and feeling. It was in the oath I took that I would, to the best of my ability, preserve, protect, and defend the Constitution of the United States. I could not take the office without taking the oath. Nor was it my view that I might take an oath to get power, and break the oath in using the power. I understood, too, that in ordinary civil administration this oath even forbade me to practically indulge my primary abstract judgment on the moral question of slavery. I had publicly declared this many times, and in many ways. And I aver that, to this day, I have done no official act in mere deference to my abstract judgment and feeling on slavery. I did understand however, that my oath to preserve the constitution to the best of my ability, imposed upon me the duty of preserving, by every indispensable means, that government—that nation—of which that constitution was the organic law. Was it possible to lose the nation, and yet preserve the constitution? By general law life *and* limb must be protected; yet often a limb must be amputated to save a life; but a life is never wisely given to save a limb. I

---

[1] Signed autograph draft, Robert Todd Lincoln Collection, Library of Congress, in *Collected Works,* VII, pp. 281–282. Albert G. Hodges, editor of the Frankfort, Kentucky, *Commonwealth,* and Archibald Dixon, former senator from Kentucky, met with Lincoln on March 26.

---

felt that measures, otherwise unconstitutional, might become lawful, by becoming indispensable to the preservation of the constitution, through the preservation of the nation. Right or wrong, I assumed this ground, and now avow it. I could not feel that, to the best of my ability, I had even tried to preserve the constitution, if, to save slavery, or any minor matter, I should permit the wreck of government, country, and Constitution all together. When, early in the war, Gen. Fremont attempted military emancipation, I forbade it, because I did not then think it an indispensable necessity. When a little later, Gen. Cameron, then Secretary of War, suggested the arming of the blacks, I objected, because I did not yet think it an indispensable necessity. When, still later, Gen. Hunter attempted military emancipation, I again forbade it, because I did not yet think the indispensable necessity had come. When, in March, and May, and July 1862 I made earnest, and successive appeals to the border states to favor compensated emancipation, I believed the indispensable necessity for military emancipation, and arming the blacks would come, unless averted by that measure. They declined the proposition; and I was, in my best judgment, driven to the alternative of either surrendering the Union, and with it, the Constitution, or of laying strong hand upon the colored element. I chose the latter. In choosing it, I hoped for greater gain than loss; but of this, I was not entirely confident. More than a year of trial now shows no loss by it in our foreign relations, none in our home popular sentiment, none in our white military force,—no loss by it any how or any where. On the contrary, it shows a gain of quite a hundred and thirty thousand soldiers, seamen, and laborers. These are palpable facts, about which, as facts, there can be no cavilling. We have the men; and we could not have had them without the measure.

["]And now let any Union man who complains of the measure, test himself by writing down in one line that he is for subduing the rebellion by force of arms; and in the next, that he is for taking these hundred and thirty thousand men from the Union side, and placing them where they would be but for the measure he condemns. If he can not face his case so stated, it is only because he can not face the truth.["]

I add a word which was not in the verbal conversation. In telling this tale I attempt no compliment to my own sagacity. I claim not to have controlled events, but confess plainly that events have controlled me. Now, at the end of three years struggle the nation's condition is not what either party, or any man devised, or expected. God alone can claim it. Whither it is tending seems plain. If God now wills the removal of a great wrong, and wills also that we of the North as well as you of the South, shall pay fairly for our complicity in that wrong, impartial history will find therein new cause to attest and revere the justice and goodness of God. Yours truly

A. LINCOLN

69

Reply to Committee Notifying Lincoln of His Renomination[1]

June 9, 1864

Gentlemen of the Committee: I will neither conceal my gratification, nor restrain the expression of my gratitude, that the Union people, through their convention, in their continued effort to save, and advance the nation, have deemed me not unworthy to remain in my present position.

I know no reason to doubt that I shall accept the nomination tendered; and yet perhaps I should not declare definitely before reading and considering what is called the Platform.[2]

---

[1] Copy, Robert Todd Lincoln Collection, Library of Congress, in *Collected Works,* VII, p. 380.

[2] The platform included the following resolutions:

.　　　.　　　.　　　.　　　.

3. *Resolved,* That as Slavery was the cause, and now constitutes the strength, of this Rebellion, and as it must be, always and everywhere, hostile to the principles of Republican Government, justice and the National safety demand its utter and complete extirpation from the soil of the Republic [applause]:—and that while we uphold and maintain the acts and proclamations by which the Government, in its own defense, has aimed a death-blow at this gigantic evil, we are in favor, furthermore, of such an amendment to the Constitution, to be made by the people in conformity with its provisions, as shall

---

I will say now, however, I approve the declaration in favor of so amending the Constitution as to prohibit slavery throughout the nation. When the people in revolt, with a hundred days of explicit notice, that they could, within those days, resume their allegiance, without the overthrow of their institution, and that they could not so resume it afterwards, elected to stand out, such amendment of the Constitution as now proposed, became a fitting, and necessary conclusion to the final success of the Union cause. Such alone can meet and cover all cavils. Now, the unconditional Union men, North and South, perceive its importance, and embrace it. In the joint names of Liberty and Union, let us labor to give it legal form, and practical effect.

---

terminate and forever prohibit the existence of slavery within the limits or the jurisdiction of the United States. [Tremendous applause, the delegates rising and waving their hats.]

. . . . .

5. *Resolved,* That we approve and applaud the practical wisdom, the unselfish patriotism and the unswerving fidelity to the Constitution and the principles of American liberty, with which ABRAHAM LINCOLN has discharged, under circumstances of unparalleled difficulty, the great duties and responsibilities of the Presidential office; that we approve and endorse, as demanded by the emergency and essential to the preservation of the nation, and as within the provisions of the Constitution, the measures and acts which he has adopted to defend the nation against its open and secret foes; that we approve, especially, the Proclamation of Emancipation, and the employment as Union soldiers of men heretofore held in slavery [applause]; and that we have full confidence in his determination to carry these and all other Constitutional measures essential to the salvation of the country into full and complete effect. [Vociferous applause.]

. . . . .

(*Proceedings of the National Union Convention* . . . [New York, 1864], pp. 57–58, in *Collected Works,* VII, pp. 381n–382n.)

70

From Charles D. Robinson[1]

August 7, 1864

I am a War Democrat, and the editor of a Democratic paper. I have sustained your Administration . . . because it is the legally constituted government. I have sustained its war policy, not because I endorsed it entire, but because it presented the only available method of putting down the rebellion. . . . It was alleged that because I and my friends sustained the Emancipation measure, we had become abolitionized. We replied that we regarded the freeing of the negroes as sound war policy, in that the depriving the South of its laborers weakened the . . . Rebellion. That was a good argument. . . . It was solid ground on which we could stand, and still maintain our position as Democrats. We were greatly comforted and strengthened also by your assurance that if you could save the Union without freeing any slave, you would do it; if you could save it by freeing the slaves, you would do it; and if you could do it by freeing some, and leaving others alone, you would also do that.

The Niagara Falls 'Peace' movement was of no importance whatever, except that it resulted in bringing out your declaration, as we understand it, that no steps can be taken towards peace . . . unless accompanied with an abandonment of slavery. This puts the whole war question on a new basis, and takes us War Democrats clear off our feet, leaving us no ground to stand upon. If we sustain the war and war policy, does it not demand the changing of our party politics?

I venture to write you this letter . . . not for the purpose of finding fault with your policy . . . but in the hope that you may suggest some interpretation of it, as will . . . make it tenable ground on which we War Democrats may stand—preserve our party consistently

---

[1] Robert Todd Lincoln Collection, Library of Congress, in *Collected Works,* VII, p. 501n. Robinson was the editor of the Greenbay, Wisconsin, *Advocate.* The letter was delivered to Lincoln by Alexander W. Randall, First Assistant Postmaster General and a former governor of Wisconsin.

---

support the government—and continue to carry also to its support those large numbers of our old political friends who have stood by us up to this time.

I beg to assure you that this is not written for the purpose of using it, or its possible reply, in a public way. And I . . . send it through my friend Gov. Randall in the belief that he will guarantee for me entire good faith.

71

To Charles D. Robinson[1]

Executive Mansion, Washington
August 17, 1864

Hon. Charles D. Robinson
My dear Sir:

Your letter of the 7th. was placed in my hand yesterday by Gov. Randall.

To me it seems plain that saying re-union and abandonment of slavery would be considered, if offered, is not saying that nothing *else* or *less* would be considered, if offered. But I will not stand upon the mere construction of language. It is true, as you remind me, that in the Greeley letter of 1862, I said: "If I could save the Union without freeing any slave I would do it; and if I could save it by freeing all the slaves I would do it; and if I could save it by freeing some, and leaving others alone I would also do that." I continued in the same letter as follows: "What I do about slavery and the colored race, I do because I believe it helps to save the Union; and what I forbear I

[1] Autograph draft, Robert Todd Lincoln Collection, Library of Congress, in *Collected Works*. VII, pp. 499–501. Lincoln probably never sent this letter.

forbear because I do not believe it would help to save the Union. I shall do less whenever I shall believe what I am doing hurts the cause; and I shall do more whenever I shall believe doing more will help the cause." All this I said in the utmost sincerety; and I am as true to the whole of it now, as when I first said it. When I afterwards proclaimed emancipation, and employed colored soldiers, I only followed the declaration just quoted from the Greeley letter that "I shall do *more* whenever I shall believe *doing* more will help the cause" The way these measures were to help the cause, was not to be by magic, or miracles, but by inducing the colored people to come bodily over from the rebel side to ours. On this point, nearly a year ago, in a letter to Mr. Conkling, made public at once, I wrote as follows: "But negroes, like other people, act upon motives. Why should they do anything for us if we will do nothing for them? If they stake their lives for us they must be prompted by the strongest motive—even the promise of freedom. And the promise, being made, must be kept." I am sure you will not, on due reflection, say that the promise being made, must be *broken* at the first opportunity. I am sure you would not desire me to say, or to leave an inference, that I am ready, whenever convenient, to join in re-enslaving those who shall have served us in consideration of our promise. As matter of morals, could such treachery by any possibility, escape the curses of Heaven, or of any good man? As matter of policy, to *announce* such a purpose, would ruin the Union cause itself. All recruiting of colored men would instantly cease, and all colored men now in our service, would instantly desert us. And rightfully too. Why should they give their lives for us, with full notice of our purpose to betray them? Drive back to the support of the rebellion the physical force which the colored people now give, and promise us, and neither the present, nor any coming administration, *can* save the Union. Take from us, and give to the enemy, the hundred and thirty, forty, or fifty thousand colored persons now serving us as soldiers, seamen, and laborers, and we can not longer maintain the contest. The party who could elect a President on a War & Slavery Restoration platform, would, of necessity, lose the colored force; and that force being lost, would be as powerless to save the Union as to do any other impossible thing. It is not a question of sentiment or taste, but one of physical force, which may be measured, and estimated as horsepower, and steam power, are measured and estimated. And by measurement, it is more than we can lose, and live. Nor can we, by discarding it, get a white force in place of it. There is a witness in every white mans bosom that he would rather go to the war having the negro to help him, than to help the enemy against him. It is not the giving of one class for another. It is simply giving a large force to the enemy, for *nothing* in return.

In addition to what I have said, allow me to remind you that no one, having control of the rebel armies, or, in fact, having any influence whatever in the rebellion, has offered, or intimated a willingness to, a restoration of the Union, in any event, or on any condition whatever. Let it be constantly borne in mind that no such offer has been made or intimated. Shall we be weak enough to allow the enemy to distract us with an abstract question which he himself refuses to present as a practical one? In the Conkling letter before mentioned, I said: "Whenever you shall have conquered all resistance to the Union, if I shall urge you to continue fighting, it will be an apt time *then* to declare that you will not fight to free negroes." I repeat this now. If Jefferson Davis wishes, for himself, or for the benefit of his friends at the North, to know what I would do if he were to offer peace and re-union, saying nothing about slavery, let him try me.

72

Speech of the Rev.
Mr. S. W. Chase, Presenting
a Bible from the Loyal Colored
Residents of Baltimore to President Lincoln[1]

September 7, 1865

MR. PRESIDENT: The loyal colored people of Baltimore have entrusted us with authority to present this Bible as a testimonial of their appreciation of your humane conduct towards the people of our race. While all others of this nation are offering their tribute of respect

[1] Washington *Daily Morning Chronicle,* September 8, 1864, in *Collected Works,* VII, p. 543n.

to you, we cannot omit suitable manifestation of ours. Since our incorporation into the American family we have been true and loyal, and we are now ready to aid in defending the country, to be armed and trained in military matters, in order to assist in protecting and defending the star-spangled banner.

Towards you, sir, our hearts will ever be warm with gratitude. We come to present to you this copy of the Holy Scriptures, as a token of respect for your active participation in furtherance of the cause of the emancipation of our race. This great event will be a matter of history. Hereafter, when our children shall ask what mean these tokens, they will be told of your worthy deeds, and will rise up and call you blessed.

The loyal colored people of this country everywhere will remember you at the Throne of Divine Grace. May the King Eternal, an allwise Providence protect and keep you, and when you pass from this world to that of eternity, may you be borne to the bosom of your Saviour and your God.

73

To Henry W. Hoffman[1]

Executive Mansion, Washington
October 10, 1864

Hon. Henry W Hoffman
My dear Sir:
A convention of Maryland has framed a new constitution for the State; a public meeting is called for this evening, at Baltimore, to aid

---

[1] Signed autograph letter, Maryland Historical Society, Baltimore, Maryland, in *Collected Works,* VIII, p. 41. Henry W. Hoffman was chairman of the committee sponsoring a mass rally in favor of the new constitution.

in securing its ratification by the people; and you ask a word from me, for the occasion. I presume the only feature of the instrument, about which there is serious controversy, is that which provides for the extinction of slavery. It needs not to be a secret, and I presume it is no secret, that I wish success to this provision. I desire it on every consideration. I wish all men to be frec. I wish the material prosperity of the already free which I feel sure the extinction of slavery would bring. I wish to see, in process of disappearing, that only thing which ever could bring this nation to civil war. I attempt no argument. Argument upon the question is already exhausted by the abler, better informed, and more immediately interested sons of Maryland herself. I only add that I shall be gratified exceedingly if the good people of the State shall, by their votes, ratify the new constitution. Yours truly

A. LINCOLN

74

Annual Message to Congress[1]

December 6, 1864

.   .   .   .   .

At the last session of Congress a proposed amendment of the Constitution abolishing slavery throughout the United States, passed the Senate, but failed for lack of the requisite two-thirds vote in the House of Representatives. Although the present is the same Congress, and nearly the same members, and without questioning the wisdom or patriotism of those who stood in opposition, I venture to recommend

---

[1] Signed document, National Archives, in *Collected Works*, VIII, pp. 149, 151–152.

the reconsideration and passage of the measure at the present session. Of course the abstract question is not changed; but an intervening election shows, almost certainly, that the next Congress will pass the measure if this does not. Hence there is only a question of *time* as to when the proposed amendment will go to the States for their action. And as it is to so go, at all events, may we not agree that the sooner the better? It is not claimed that the election has imposed a duty on members to change their views or their votes, any further than, as an additional element to be considered, their judgment may be affected by it. It is the voice of the people now, for the first time, heard upon the question. In a great national crisis, like ours, unanimity of action among those seeking a common end is very desirable—almost indispensable. And yet no approach to such unanimity is attainable, unless some deference shall be paid to the will of the majority, simply because it is the will of the majority. In this case the common end is the maintenance of the Union; and, among the means to secure that end, such will, through the election, is most clearly declared in favor of such constitutional amendment.

.　　.　　.　　.　　.

The national resources, then, are unexhausted, and, as we believe, inexhaustible. The public purpose to re-establish and maintain the national authority is unchanged, and, as we believe, unchangeable. The manner of continuing the effort remains to choose. On careful consideration of all the evidence accessible it seems to me that no attempt at negotiation with the insurgent leader could result in any good. He would accept nothing short of severance of the Union— precisely what we will not and cannot give. His declarations to this effect are explicit and oft-repeated. He does not attempt to deceive us. He affords us no excuse to deceive ourselves. He cannot voluntarily reaccept the Union; we cannot voluntarily yield it. Between him and us the issue is distinct, simple, and inflexible. It is an issue which can only be tried by war, and decided by victory. If we yield, we are beaten; if the Southern people fail him, he is beaten. Either way, it would be the victory and defeat following war. What is true, however, of him who heads the insurgent cause, is not necessarily true of those who follow. Although he cannot reaccept the Union, they can. Some of them, we know, already desire peace and reunion. The number of such may increase. They can, at any moment, have peace simply by laying down their arms and submitting to the national authority under the Constitution. After so much, the government could not, if it would, maintain war against them. The loyal people would not sustain or allow it. If questions should remain, we would adjust them by the peaceful means of legislation, conference, courts, and votes, operating only in constitutional and lawful channels. . . .

. . . . .

In presenting the abandonment of armed resistance to the national authority on the part of the insurgents, as the only indispensable condition to ending the war on the part of the government, I retract nothing heretofore said as to slavery. I repeat the declaration made a year ago, that "while I remain in my present position I shall not attempt to retract or modify the emancipation proclamation, nor shall I return to slavery any person who is free by the terms of that proclamation, or by any of the Acts of Congress." If the people should, by whatever mode or means, make it an Executive duty to re-enslave such persons, another, and not I, must be their instrument to perform it.

In stating a single condition of peace, I mean simply to say that the war will cease on the part of the government, whenever it shall have ceased on the part of those who began it.

ABRAHAM LINCOLN

75

To William H. Seward [1]

Executive Mansion, Washington
January 31, 1865

Hon. William H. Seward.
Secretary of State.
You will proceed to Fortress-Monroe, Virginia, there to meet,

---

[1] A copy of this document was included in a series of documents concerning negotiations with Confederate agents which Lincoln submitted to Congress. Autograph document, Robert Todd Lincoln Collection, Library of Congress, in *Collected Works,* VIII, pp. 279–280.

and informally confer with Messrs. Stephens, Hunter, and Camp-bell.[2] . . .

You will make known to them that three things are indispensable, towit:

1. The restoration of the National authority throughout all the States.
2. No receding by the Executive of the United States, on the Slavery question, from the position assumed thereon, in the late Annual Message to Congress, and on preceding documents.
3. No cessation of hostilities short of an end of the war, and the disbanding of all forces hostile to the government.

You will inform them that all propositions of theirs, not inconsistent with the above, will be considered and passed upon, in a spirit of sincere liberality.

You will hear all they may choose to say, and report it to me.

You will not assume to definitely consummate any thing. Yours
&c   ABRAHAM LINCOLN.

---

[2] Alexander Stephens, J. A. Campbell, and R. M. T. Hunter had been appointed by Jefferson Davis to discuss peace terms. This peace move proved abortive.

76

Response to a Serenade[1]

February 1, 1865

The President said he supposed the passage through Congress of the Constitutional amendment for the abolishment of Slavery through-

---

[1] New York *Tribune,* February 3, 1865, in *Collected Works,* VIII, pp. 254–255.

out the United States, was the occasion to which he was indebted for the honor of this call. [Applause.] The occasion was one of congratulation to the country and to the whole world. But there is a task yet before us—to go forward and consummate by the votes of the States that which Congress so nobly began yesterday. [Applause and cries—"They will do it," &c.] He had the honor to inform those present that Illinois had already to-day done the work. [Applause.] Maryland was about half through; but he felt proud that Illinois was a little ahead. He thought this measure was a very fitting if not an indispensable adjunct to the winding up of the great difficulty. He wished the reunion of all the States perfected and so effected as to remove all causes of disturbance in the future; and to attain this end it was necessary that the original disturbing cause should, if possible, be rooted out. He thought all would bear him witness that he had never shrunk from doing all that he could to eradicate Slavery by issuing an emancipation proclamation. [Applause.] But that proclamation falls far short of what the amendment will be when fully consummated. A question might be raised whether the proclamation was legally valid. It might be added that it only aided those who came into our lines and that it was inoperative as to those who did not give themselves up, or that it would have no effect upon the children of the slaves born hereafter. In fact it would be urged that it did not meet the evil. But this amendment is a King's cure for all the evils. [Applause.] It winds the whole thing up. He would repeat that it was the fitting if not indispensable adjunct to the consummation of the great game we are playing. He could not but congratulate all present, himself, the country and the whole world upon this great moral victory.

77

To the Senate and House of Representatives[1]

February 5, 1865

Fellow citizens of the Senate, and
House of Representatives.

I respectfully recommend that a Joint Resolution, substantially as follows, be adopted so soon as practicable, by your honorable bodies.

"Resolved by the Senate and House of Representatives, of the United States of America in congress assembled: That the President of the United States is hereby empowered, in his discretion, to pay four hundred millions of dollars to the States of Alabama, Arkansas, Delaware, Florida, Georgia, Kentucky, Louisiana, Maryland Mississippi, Missouri, North Carolina, South Carolina, Tennessee, Texas, Virginia, and West-Virginia, in the manner, and on the conditions following, towit: The payment to be made in six per cent government bonds, and to be distributed among said States *pro rata* on their respective slave populations, as shown by the census of 1860; and no part of said sum to be paid unless all resistance to the national authority shall be abandoned and cease, on or before the first day of April next; and upon such abandonment and ceasing of resistance, one half of said sum to be paid in manner aforesaid, and the remaining half to be paid only upon the amendment of the national constitution recently proposed by congress, becoming valid law, on or before the first day of July next, by the action thereon of the requisite number of States"

The adoption of such resolution is sought with a view to embody it, with other propositions, in a proclamation looking to peace and re-union.

Whereas a Joint Resolution has been adopted by congress in the words following, towit

---

[1] Autograph draft, Robert Todd Lincoln Collection, Library of Congress, in *Collected Works*, VIII, pp. 260–261.

Now therefore I, Abraham Lincoln, President of the United States, do proclaim, declare, and make known, that on the conditions therein stated, the power conferred on the Executive in and by said Joint Resolution, will be fully exercised; that war will cease, and armies be reduced to a basis of peace; that all political offences will be pardoned; that all property, except slaves, liable to confiscation or forfeiture, will be released therefrom, except in cases of intervening interests of third parties; and that liberality will be recommended to congress upon all points not lying within executive control.

[Endorsement]

Feb. 5. 1865

To-day these papers, which explain themselves, were drawn up and submitted to the Cabinet & unanamously disapproved by them.

A LINCOLN

78

To John Glenn[1]

Executive Mansion, Washington
February 7, 1865

"Cypher"
Lt. Col. Glenn.
Commanding Post at
Henderson, Ky.

Complaint is made to me that you are forcing negroes into the Military service, and even torturing them—riding them on rails and

---

[1] Signed autograph letter, National Archives, in *Collected Works,* VIII, p. 266.

---

the like—to extort their consent. I hope this may be a mistake. The like must not be done by you, or any one under you. You must not force negroes any more than white men. Answer me on this.

A. LINCOLN

79

Second Inaugural Address[1]

March 4, 1865

At this second appearing to take the oath of the presidential office, there is less occasion for an extended address than there was at the first. Then a statement, somewhat in detail, of a course to be pursued, seemed fitting and proper. Now, at the expiration of four years, during which public declarations have been constantly called forth on every point and phase of the great contest which still absorbs the attention, and engrosses the enerergies [sic] of the nation, little that is new could be presented. The progress of our arms, upon which all else chiefly depends, is as well known to the public as to myself; and it is, I trust, reasonably satisfactory and encouraging to all. With high hope for the future, no prediction in regard to it is ventured.

On the occasion corresponding to this four years ago, all thoughts were anxiously directed to an impending civil-war. All dreaded it—all sought to avert it. While the inaugeral address was being delivered from this place, devoted altogether to *saving* the Union without war, insurgent agents were in the city seeking to *destroy* it without war—seeking to dissol[v]e the Union, and divide effects, by negotiation. Both parties deprecated war; but one of them

---

[1] Autograph document, Library of Congress, in *Collected Works*, VIII, pp. 332–333.

---

would *make* war rather than let the nation survive; and the other would *accept* war rather than let it perish. And the war came.

One eighth of the whole population were colored slaves, not distributed generally over the Union, but localized in the Southern part of it. These slaves constituted a peculiar and powerful interest. All knew that this interest was, somehow, the cause of the war. To strengthen, perpetuate, and extend this interest was the object for which the insurgents would rend the Union, even by war; while the government claimed no right to do more than to restrict the territorial enlargement of it. Neither party expected for the war, the magnitude, or the duration, which it has already attained. Neither anticipated that the *cause* of the conflict might cease with, or even before, the conflict itself should cease. Each looked for an easier triumph, and a result less fundamental and astounding. Both read the same Bible, and pray to the same God; and each invokes His aid against the other. It may seem strange that any men should dare to ask a just God's assistance in wringing their bread from the sweat of other men's faces; but let us judge not that we be not judged. The prayers of both could not be answered; that of neither has been answered fully. The Almighty has His own purposes. "Woe unto the world because of offences! for it must needs be that offences come; but woe to that man by whom the offence cometh!" If we shall suppose that American Slavery is one of those offences which, in the providence of God, must needs come, but which, having continued through His appointed time, He now wills to remove, and that He gives to both North and South, this terrible war, as the woe due to those by whom the offence came, shall we discern therein any departure from those divine attributes which the believers in a Living God always ascribe to Him? Fondly do we hope—fervently do we pray—that this mighty scourge of war may speedily pass away. Yet, if God wills that it continue, until all the wealth piled by the bond-man's two hundred and fifty years of unrequited toil shall be sunk, and until every drop of blood drawn with the lash, shall be paid by another drawn with the sword, as was said three thousand years ago, so still it must be said "the judgments of the Lord, are true and righteous altogether"

With malice toward none; with charity for all; with firmness in the right, as God gives us to see the right, let us strive on to finish the work we are in; to bind up the nation's wounds; to care for him who shall have borne the battle, and for his widow, and his orphan—to do all which may achieve and cherish a just, and a lasting peace, among ourselves, and with all nations.

80

Salmon P. Chase to Abraham Lincoln[1]

April 11, 1865

When all mankind are congratulating you, one voice, heard or not, is of little account; but I add mine.

I am very anxious about the future; and most about the principles which are to govern reconstruction; for as these principles are sound or unsound, so will be the work and its results.

You have no time to read a long letter, nor have I time to write one; so I will be brief.

.   .   .   .   .

The easiest and safest way seems to me to be the enrollment of the loyal citizens without regard to complexion, and encouragement and support to them in the reorganization of State governments under constitutions securing suffrage to all citizens of proper age and unconvicted of crime. This, you know, has long been my opinion. It is confirmed by observation more and more.

This way is recommended by its simplicity, facility, and, above all, justice. It will be hereafter counted equally a crime and a folly if the colored loyalists of the rebel States are left to the control of restored rebels, not likely, in that case, to be either wise or just, until taught both wisdom and justice by new calamities.

The application of this principle to Louisiana is made somewhat difficult by the organization which has already taken place; but, happily, the Constitution authorizes the Legislature to extend the right of suffrage; and it is not to be doubted that, on a suggestion from the national authorities, that its extension to colored citizens, on equal terms with white citizens, is believed to be essential to the future

---

[1] J. W. Schuckers, *The Life and Public Services of Salmon Portland Chase* . . . (New York: D. Appleton and Co., 1874), pp. 514–515.

---

tranquillity of the country as well as just in itself, the Legislature will promptly act in the desired direction.

What reaches me of the condition of things in Louisiana impresses me strongly with the belief that this extension will be of the greatest benefit to the whole population.

The same result can be secured in Arkansas by an amendment of the State constitution, or, what would be better, I think, by a new convention, the members of which should be elected by the loyal citizens, without distinction of color. To all the other States, the general principle may be easily applied.

I most respectfully but most earnestly commend these matters to your attention God gives you a great place and a great opportunity. May He guide you in the use of them!

·   ·   ·   ·   ·

81

Last Public Address[1]

April 11, 1865

We meet this evening, not in sorrow, but in gladness of heart. The evacuation of Petersburg and Richmond, and the surrender of the principal insurgent army, give hope of a righteous and speedy peace whose joyous expression can not be restrained. . . .

By these recent successes the re-inauguration of the national authority—reconstruction—which had had a large share of thought from the first, is pressed much more closely upon our attention. It is

---

[1] Photocopy of autograph document, Abraham Lincoln Association, Springfield, Illinois, in *Collected Works,* VIII, pp. 399–404.

fraught with great difficulty. Unlike the case of a war between independent nations, there is no authorized organ for us to treat with. No one man has authority to give up the rebellion for any other man. We simply must begin with, and mould from, disorganized and discordant elements. Nor is it a small additional embarrassment that we, the loyal people, differ among ourselves as to the mode, manner, and means of reconstruction.

As a general rule, I abstain from reading the reports of attacks upon myself, wishing not to be provoked by that to which I can not properly offer an answer. In spite of this precaution, however, it comes to my knowledge that I am much censured for some supposed agency in setting up, and seeking to sustain, the new State Government of Louisiana. In this I have done just so much as, and no more than, the public knows. In the Annual Message of Dec. 1863 and accompanying Proclamation, I presented *a* plan of re-construction (as the phrase goes) which, I promised, if adopted by any State, should be acceptable to, and sustained by, the Executive government of the nation. I distinctly stated that this was not the only plan which might possibly be acceptable; and I also distinctly protested that the Executive claimed no right to say when, or whether members should be admitted to seats in Congress from such States. This plan was, in advance, submitted to the then Cabinet, and distinctly approved by every member of it. One of them suggested that I should then, and in that connection, apply the Emancipation Proclamation to the theretofore excepted parts of Virginia and Louisiana; that I should drop the suggestion about apprenticeship for freed-people, and that I should omit the protest against my own power, in regard to the admission of members to Congress; but even he approved every part and parcel of the plan which has since been employed or touched by the action of Louisiana. The new constitution of Louisiana, declaring emancipation for the whole State, practically applies the Proclamation to the part previously excepted. It does not adopt apprenticeship for freed-people; and it is silent, as it could not well be otherwise, about the admission of members to Congress. So that, as it applies to Louisiana, every member of the Cabinet fully approved the plan. The Message went to Congress, and I received many commendations of the plan, written and verbal; and not a single objection to it, from any professed emancipationist, came to my knowledge, until after the news reached Washington that the people of Louisiana had begun to move in accordance with it. From about July 1862, I had corresponded with different persons, supposed to be interested, seeking a reconstruction of a State government for Louisiana. When the Message of 1863, with the plan before mentioned, reached New-Orleans, Gen. Banks wrote me that he was confident the people, with his military co-operation, would reconstruct, substantially on that plan. I wrote him, and some of them to try it; they tried it, and the result is known. Such only has been my agency in getting up the Louisiana government. As to sustaining it, my promise is out, as before stated. But, as bad promises are better broken than kept, I shall treat this as a bad promise, and break it, whenever I shall be convinced that keeping it is adverse to the public interest. But I have not yet been so convinced.

.   .   .   .   .

The amount of constituency, so to to [sic] speak, on which the new Louisiana government rests, would be more satisfactory to all, if it contained fifty, thirty, or even twenty thousand, instead of only about twelve thousand, as it does. It is also unsatisfactory to some that the elective franchise is not given to the colored man. I would myself prefer that it were now conferred on the very intelligent, and on those who serve our cause as soldiers. Still the question is not whether the Louisiana government, as it stands, is quite all that is desirable. The question is "Will it be wiser to take it as it is, and help to improve it; or to reject, and disperse it?" "Can Louisiana be brought into proper practical relation with the Union *sooner* by *sustaining,* or by *discarding* her new State Government?"

Some twelve thousand voters in the heretofore slave-state of Louisiana have sworn allegiance to the Union, assumed to be the rightful political power of the State, held elections, organized a State government, adopted a free-state constitution, giving the benefit of public schools equally to black and white, and empowering the Legislature to confer the elective franchise upon the colored man. Their Legislature has already voted to ratify the constitutional amendment recently passed by Congress, abolishing slavery throughout the nation. These twelve thousand persons are thus fully committed to the Union, and to perpetual freedom in the state—committed to the very things, and nearly all the things the nation wants—and they ask the nations recognition, and it's assistance to make good their committal. Now, if we reject, and spurn them, we do our utmost to disorganize and disperse them. We in effect say to the white men "You are worthless, or worse—we will neither help you, nor be helped by you." To the blacks we say "This cup of liberty which these, your old masters, hold to your lips, we will dash from you, and leave you to the chances of gathering the spilled and scattered contents in some vague and undefined when, where, and how." If this course, discouraging and paralyzing both white and black, has any tendency to bring Louisiana into proper practical relations with the Union, I have, so far, been unable to perceive it. If, on the contrary, we recognize, and sustain the new government of Louisiana the converse of all this is made true. We encourage the hearts, and nerve the arms of the twelve thousand to adhere to their work, and argue for it, and proselyte for it, and fight for it, and feed it, and grow it, and ripen it to a complete success. The colored man too, in seeing all united for him, is inspired with vigilance, and energy, and daring, to the same end. Grant that he desires the elective franchise, will he not attain it sooner by saving the already advanced steps toward it, than by running backward over them? Concede that the new government of Louisiana is only to what it should be as the egg is to the fowl, we shall sooner have the fowl by hatching the egg than by smashing it? Again, if we reject Louisiana, we also reject one vote in favor of the proposed amendment to the national constitution. To meet this proposition, it has been argued that no more than three fourths of those States which have not attempted secession are necessary to validly ratify the amendment. I do not commit myself against this, further than to say that such a ratification would be questionable, and sure to be persistently questioned; while a ratification by three fourths of all the States would be unquestioned and unquestionable.

I repeat the question. "Can Louisiana be brought into proper practical relation with the Union *sooner* by *sustaining* or by *discarding* her new State Government?

. . . . .

Suggestions for Further Research

The following primary sources are useful for further research.
The most valuable source for a student of Lincoln is the monumental edition of the Lincoln papers produced by the Abraham Lin-

coln Association: *The Collected Works of Abraham Lincoln,* Roy P. Basler *et al.,* eds. (9 vols., New Brunswick, N. J.: Rutgers University Press, 1953). For a good look at Lincoln's wartime decisions, see two outstanding diaries of his cabinet members: *Inside Lincoln's Cabinet: The Civil War Diaries of Salmon P. Chase,* David Donald, ed. (New York: Longmans, Green and Co., 1954), and *Diary of Gideon Welles,* Howard K. Beale, ed. (3 vols., New York: W. W. Norton & Co., 1960). A judicious collection of documents which includes valuable material on Lincoln as viewed by his Black contemporaries is *The Negro's Civil War,* James M. McPherson, ed. (New York: Random House, 1967). *Union Pamphlets of the Civil War, 1861–1865,* Frank B. Freidel, ed. (2 vols., Cambridge, Mass.: Harvard University Press, 1967) is a valuable source of information on contemporary public opinion. A convenient collection of newspaper opinion at a crucial period is *Northern Editorials on Secession,* Howard C. Perkins, ed. (2 vols., Gloucester, Mass.: Peter Smith, 1964). Students who have access to contemporary newspapers and periodicals will not only find valuable clues to American attitudes on race, but will share with other historians the joys of the hunt for the significant documents.